SILENT ABUSE

a book by

SALLY JAYNE

'No one saves us but ourselves. No one can and no one may.
We ourselves must walk the path.'
[Source: Buddha]

Copyright © 2025 Sally Jayne Eastland All rights reserved

The characters and events portrayed in this book are fictitious. Any similarity to real persons, living or dead, is coincidental and not intended by the author.

No part of this book may be reproduced, or stored in a retrieval system, or transmitted in any form or by any means, electronic, mechanical, photocopying, recording, or otherwise, without express written permission of the publisher.

ISBN: 9798287847548

Back Cover design by: Art Painter / Photo by Helen James
Front Cover design by: Marck Studzinski for Unsplash

WITH LOVE & GRATITUDE TO:

My daughter Daisy for always believing in me regardless of where my pathway has taken me. To my much beloved paternal Grandma Theresa, who showered me with love, cuddles & cake. To the father of my daughter for loving the young girl that I was. To my parents whose Soul's struggled endlessly. To Graham for all the love you gave. To my wonderful friends new and old who help me see the Light within; for the friends who have guided or keep turning up no matter what —Carol, Bev, Amanda, Tracy, Natasha, Caroline, Jon, Sam, Helen, and Niki.

To every client who has supported my therapy work, which has assisted my own growth while keeping the wolf from the door.

To every teacher who has guided me on this pathway. To the work of the late Dr Wayne Dyer whose books saved my life and helped me to reconnect with faith.

To the beautiful soul I call Manuel Angel

To my Holy Father

List of Contents:

Introduction:
Signs & Synchronicities   page 7-33

The First 20 Years:
Chapter 1	Red Flags:	Love Bombing/Quick to Commit	page	34-53
Chapter 2	Red Flags:	Gaslighting/Isolation from Others	page	54-68
Chapter 3	Red Flag:	Stonewalling	page	69-82
Chapter 4	Red Flags:	Excessive Need for Admiration/ Grandiose Self Image/Entitlement	page	83-103
Chapter 5	Red Flag:	Manipulation	page	104-123
Chapter 6	Red Flags:	Exploitation/Devaluation	page	124-140
Chapter 7	Red Flags:	Jealousy/Possessiveness	page	141-151
Chapter 8	Red Flags:	Lack of Accountability/ Quick to Anger	page	152-161
Chapter 9	Red Flag:	Lies	page	162-174
Chapter 10	Red Flags:	Twists Conversations/Plays Victim	page	175-189

The Last Two Years:
Chapter 11   The Journey to I AM: the Awakening   page 190-206

Appendix   page 207-209
About the Author   page 210

PREFACE

'A narcissist is someone who demands you to give up everything – your dreams, your desires, your goals, your family, your identity – in order to be their nothing. They require you to sacrifice your very essence, your autonomy, and your individuality to feed their insatiable ego and satisfy their need for control. They'll promise the world but deliver only emptiness. They'll flatter and charm you, only to crush and discard you. They'll make you feel like you're the centre of their universe, but ultimately, you'll just be another orbiting satellite, trapped in their gravitational pull. Their love is a suffocating shroud, a strangling vine that chokes the life out of you. Their attention is a toxin, a poison that infects your soul and leaves you gasping for air. Their affection is a noose, a tightening grip that slowly strangles your sense of self. Don't be fooled by their grandiose gestures and sweet nothings.

Don't be seduced by their charm and charisma. See them for what they are – a black hole of neediness, a void of emptiness, an abyss of selfishness. And remember, you deserve to be someone's everything not their nothing.'

[FB post: I Deserve Better]

A JOURNEY TO SELF:

For the sake of my own well-being, I took a leap of faith to leave a 20-year relationship, because I was guided by angels and God, my Holy Father to do so. I hadn't connected with either for a long time, but they suddenly made themselves known to me via a series of strange synchronicities that were difficult to ignore.
Because of them, I came to realise that I was the victim of silent abuse; two decades of psychological torment that fuelled fear, anxiety, and lack of self-worth. Leaving was probably one of the most terrifying things I have ever done; I was middle-aged, jobless, broke, and living in a country where I couldn't speak the language: but I did it anyway, because like I say, I was told to jump.

Fast forward one year. I'm driving my bright blue car up a winding road; I'm heading to work, where I will chop vegetables and wash dishes. The sun is out, and the sky is blue and all around are mountains, open planes, and fields full of orange, lemon, fig, olive, and almond trees. Above, an aircraft flies: I imagine it full of people who are arriving to Almeria on holiday. I visualise myself sat on the plane and what thoughts I would have; I'd be looking out of that window at the mountains, trees and also the blue car driving along the winding road and wishing with every ounce of my heart that that life was mine.

Sally Jayne xx

INTRODUCTION

Signs & Synchronicities

What led me to ring Walt for relationship advice wasn't a decision that was made overnight. It was a choice that came after months of a niggling feeling that something wasn't right in my marriage to Ian. It was a feeling that was so uncomfortable that I didn't feel able to discuss my true emotions with even my closest girlfriends; I was fearful that if my sentiments were unfounded that it would leave them with a lingering negative impression of my husband.

Thus, it was more discreet to speak to Walt. Compared to my girlfriends, I knew that as a male friend he would give me solid advice that wasn't based on the quirks of female solidarity. I knew that he would be able to handle my feelings of confusion; the basis of my concerns seemed very deep but were also shrouded in uncertainty. The ambiguity of my emotions created a sense that I was toying with something that was potentially damaging. I realised that mud could stick and that I couldn't afford for my life to accidentally unfold. I had to be very cautious.

Assisting people in my situation was Walt's profession. His work as a police officer with the Domestic Violence Unit (DVU), meant that he'd seen and heard it all before. I knew that I could speak to him without judgement and if my worries were baseless then I could just get on with making my marriage work without fear of repercussions and the loose lips of protective friends.

Even though I knew that Walt would be highly professional and supportive, it still felt somewhat extreme to call him. He had a serious job dealing with grave situations and I felt that I had no right to steal his time with what could prove to be just overreactive emotions.

I questioned how I could even begin to think that the niggling feelings I'd been experiencing could ever be linked to anything unsettling. But then there was this other part of me, the intuitive side, that kind of knew that I had to call him. That I had to trust I was being almost pushed or guided to do it.

Nonetheless, I didn't expect the conversation to unfold in the way that it did. I imagined Walt to advise me that marriages were always difficult, especially after 20-years and to tell me to work through the rough patches. But he didn't. Instead, a casual conversation turned into a more formal off-the-record, police interview. I wasn't prepared for him to advise me to,

"Get out, while you still can", adding,

"It will only get worse."

I believed in love and if anyone had said to me that I would up and leave Ian after two decades, I would have thought them mad. I truly believed that I couldn't live without my husband, which I felt defined the deep level of love I had for him. Therefore, I wasn't looking for change or to end my relationship; I planned to be with Ian until the very end. I had simply wanted Walt's professional reassurance that everything I'd been feeling was normal, but it didn't work out that way.

Instead, I took a leap of faith to trust in the sequence of events, the sense of being guided, that had led me into making the phone call. An order of incidents that seemed to unfold in a way that felt like synchronicity; an endless series of inexplicable signs that became difficult to ignore and were at times too profound and detailed to be viewed as coincidence. Guidance that has led me to believe that it was outside influences that kept catching my attention; notifying me that something was very wrong in my marriage and that I must start paying attention.

The more I labelled certain events as 'spiritual signs', a form of Divine intervention, the more I naturally began to question my own sanity. After all, Ian often referred to me as 'crazy' and I tended to see myself from his point of view, even when he claimed that the reference was one of playful endearment. I was prone to worrying that he could be right, that I could be mad, and I had my reasons for thinking this way. I also knew that I was capable of seeking comfort in spiritual beliefs; I was well versed on many esoteric subjects and had been reading books of this genre for the entirety of our relationship. I had shared my views and beliefs with Ian; a trait that I came to believe had made me vulnerable and weak, and yet, it has proved to be one of my greatest strengths.

Nonetheless, the more I resisted and questioned the signs, the more they came. It was as if, God, Holy Father, the One Consciousness, whatever you or I want to refer to the energy that exists within and around us, was conspiring to ensure that I couldn't keep ignoring Him. It is my preference to refer to a Him; it is personal to me, a deep-rooted need for my vision of God to be my Holy Father, for I have come to believe that this beautiful and Divine energy comes to us in whatever form we need for healing on this journey. Thus, my path has led to forming a spiritual relationship with what I now refer to as my Holy Father; but it did take some time to get to that point.

Thus, the signs came in various forms. The first significant indication that something otherworldly was occurring, was seeing repetitive numbers. Numbers that I've learnt to accept as 'angelic numbers'. I believe that universally we can communicate with Spirit and other energy forms in a way that both parties agree. Therefore, for example, if someone teaches that Christ energy can appear as a golden ray of light, and I accept this, I have agreed and invited for that connection, or sign, to occur in my life. I have agreed to this as a form of spiritual communication.

So, as soon as I accepted that multiplications of the number 11, which I acknowledged as an angelic number were a sign of communication, the more that they would appear. Every time I looked at a clock, the mileage on the car or glanced up to see a car number plate, date, or temperature gauge, I would see the time was 11:11 or 22:22, the mileage was 21,111.11 or a number plate had 1122 or 2233 for example. It was endless.

I didn't spend my day looking for these numbers, I would be engaged in some other activity and then I would get this feeling, an instinct to look at the clock and there the numbers would be. Not just once or twice, but on some days, over 20 times: I began to screen shot the numbers on my mobile phone.

It happened so frequently, I began to notice what my thoughts were at the time, and invariably, I would be thinking about Ian. I would be contemplating something hurtful he'd said, words that I would be desperate to dismiss as another one of his so-called jokes. Usually, his remarks were about my weight and appearance. He also made frequent comparisons between myself and his late-partner Eva, which initially I put down to grief.

Nonetheless, I didn't understand what was happening to me. I couldn't make sense of the reoccurring number patterns and why I felt a growing unease whenever I was with the man, I deemed I would love till the end of time.

But the numbers kept coming, even to the point of a voice speaking to me in the middle of the night, telling me to "wake up, look at the clock." And sure enough, time and time again, there would be an angelic number, 1:11, 2:22: till eventually it simply became impossible to ignore that whatever crazy scenario I'd found myself in, I couldn't escape the fact that my relationship with Ian, no longer felt right.

Once I began to connect with the angelic numbers and use them as a form of emotional life compass, which I would invariably and often question regardless of the frequency of evidence, other synchronicities or unusual, inexplicable events became evident. The next thing I noticed, was an unusual connection with animals, specifically the Ibex, which is a form of wild goat, commonly found in the mountains of Europe, Asia, and north-eastern Africa.

In the two decades I'd known Ian, he had always been self-employed, which meant that he often worked from home. Even after our move to Spain, and Ian reaching retirement age, he was driven by the desire to become a self-made millionaire, which over the years, progressed to billionaire.

While Ian worked, I would prepare food and refreshments; set lunch out on the shaded garden table, where I would sit and wait to eat until Ian joined me. I spent a lot of time sitting alone. It was during these moments that I noticed the strange interaction with Ibex. While seeing one of these wonderful creatures isn't unusual in the mountains of Almeria, it was the intensity of the interaction I had with a female Ibex that caught my attention. We would engage in eye contact for what felt like tens of seconds; she would move her head as if strangely acknowledging me. Sometimes she would appear with her two young, but mostly on her own.

Obviously, I cannot be sure if it was the same female Ibex who returned each time, but her calm and curious behaviour toward me suggested we had become familiar to one another. She would peer over the wall or stand at the end of the driveway, and we would spend seconds gazing at each other. I felt like she really saw me, and I appreciated that this normally timid creature seemed to know that I would never harm her. It was a true honour to engage in this way: a wonderful Divine gift from above.

In those precious moments, my senses began to be awoken. I started to see myself as much more than the insignificant person I felt that I'd become. I felt trusted and seen. I opened myself to feeling reconnected with my own gentleness and sensitive awareness, I began to see the beauty within my own personality. I was changing within and at the same time, the continuation of the angelic numbers was making me more aware of being part of something much bigger than just my isolated singular life.

Yet whenever she arrived and saw that I was sitting with Ian, her demeanour was always anxious and scared. She would look at me and then at him before fearfully disappearing up the rocky mountainside until next time.

Of course, Ian never noticed, he was usually scrolling through emails on his phone. In my silent reverie, I felt that her reaction to Ian was an omen, which prompted me to start gauging my internal reaction to how I felt emotionally, mentally, and physically when in Ian's presence. I began to observe how my body responded to his narrative.

Shortly after this, another synchronicity came into play, when my passport went missing for weeks.

The decision to move to Spain had been made by Ian, who at the time, was running away from the fallout of a failed UK business that he ran with his brother Paul. The collapse had resulted in the forced sale of our home in Devon, which had left us with limited resources. Within a week of losing our home, our plans to rebuild a new life closer to London came to a sudden halt when the entire world was affected by the COVID pandemic. This was followed by the UK voting to leave the EU via what became known as Brexit: neither COVID nor Brexit were to blame for the company's failure; the demise had been coming for a number of years.

Ian lived what I would call a high risk strategy lifestyle. He always claimed that he couldn't do 9-5 job; that was for 'ordinary' people. Thus, when our plans for a revised future, were scuppered due to two life changing events, global and economically, he insisted on investing what little resources we had into a similar scheme to the one that had caused the downfall of his business. Needless to say, I didn't like the plan. In spite of this, Spain was meant to be a new start for the two of us: it was to offer Ian a fresh playground to rebuild a new business, which would initially be funded by the dividends earned from the newest investment scheme.

Over time, Ian's general goal was to create his billionaire and luxury lifestyle fantasy. However, within months of arriving in Spain, Ian soon felt that he'd made a mistake; alongside a pandemic, he had not given any real consideration to his lack of contacts and the language barrier. I think he truly believed that everyone would speak English and that if he looked the part, wearing his expensive suits and handmade shirts, that everything would just slot into place. But the world was not only changing but it had changed overnight. The added disadvantage was the location; the hot spot for the kind of contacts Ian wanted to meet, were roughly 3-hours away in Marbella.

As a result, while Ian would have preferred to have avoided the UK business fallout, by burying his head in the sand; he realised that his dreams were more likely to come to fruition if he returned to the UK. However, I didn't want to go back to England; I had fallen in love with Spain and felt a deep calling to make Almeria my forever home.

Yet, I felt powerless to express my wishes. If Ian insisted that we return to the UK, then that is exactly what would happen, and at the time, Ian was not suggesting any timespan for the return trip, it was for an indefinite amount of time. Therefore, if we were to leave Spain then our application for residential status would be cancelled.

Nonetheless, both of our passports needed to be renewed prior to any travel. We used a professional service that did the application on our behalf to ensure that the passports could be tracked and delivered via a quicker and respected courier. The application for two new passports was made and all we had to do was wait.

Ian's passport arrived within six weeks and mine went missing. According to the tracking service, it was 'in the system', but it didn't arrive. The Universe had other plans for me; I wasn't going anywhere. Reluctantly, Ian put the trip to the UK on hold while we awaited my passport. It was a tense time.

The longer the wait, the more it allowed Ian time to find fault in everything relating to the Spanish lifestyle. His main focus was the lack of luxury rental accommodation in the region we resided; he began to refer to our lifestyle as *third world* existence and complained at the general lack of opulence in terms of local hotels, restaurants, and gentlemen's retail clothing. The more days that passed, the more irritated he got and the more he wanted to return to the UK.

The uncertainty on whether we would return to the UK permanently, began to make me feel unwell. I suffered from anxiety, which presented itself as severe panic attacks. Every day, Ian would talk about the UK business fallout and was suggesting that a group action was being taken out against the company he ran with his brother Paul, which he claimed, could lead to court cases and imprisonment. This caused my anxiety to reach an all-time high; I couldn't sleep, and I cried, when alone, most days.

Additionally, I would seek comfort in food, which resulted in me piling on weight. I also started to experience severe pain in my feet, which made walking very difficult.

One day, Ian accidentally walked into a glass door. Stunned, he fell to the floor and injured his head, elbow, and hip. It was awful to witness, and I hated to see him in pain or injured. However, the incident fed his campaign for an imminent and permanent return to the UK, where he claimed that he would at least be able to live in safer and more luxurious conditions.

The clock was ticking. If I, and it would be up to me, didn't find a suitable long-term rental home, we would be returning to the UK for good. I didn't want to leave, but it was only a matter of time before my passport would arrive, then it would be game over for a life in Spain.

The day after Ian walked into the glass door, we met with friends, Anita, and Malcolm, for coffee, at a local bar. Oddly, we'd both known Anita prior to moving to Spain when living back in the UK; we met her via her business, but had never had the opportunity to meet Malcolm, until relocating overseas.

We first became acquainted with Anita, while living in a lavish rental property in Hampshire. At the time, we still had a base home in Devon, but Ian had wanted to be closer to the 'money', which meant living within an easy commute distance to London. For this purpose, Ian regularly rented 'showcase' properties, including the Hampshire pad, to impress and attract potential business opportunities.

When Ian and I first met, I was a single parent to my daughter, Lauren, from a previous marriage. Therefore, throughout our relationship, if we were to remain together as a family unit, then any relocation would need to take Lauren's educational needs into consideration. If this wasn't possible, then my priority as a parent, was to stay with my daughter in the southwest.

As a family unit we moved from Devon to Hampshire, and it was while renting in this area, that we met Anita. At the time, I was still relatively new to exploring my own spiritual beliefs and I was excited when I got to meet people with similar interests. Our initial rental home sat on the border with Sussex and Surrey, in what is referred to as the *Golden Triangle*. Within easy driving distance, I made friends with two like-minded women, one of which was Anita.

Anita used to own a wonderful shop in Sussex, which sold anything from crystals and dreamcatchers to silver jewellery and esoteric books. I loved visiting her store, which also had a treatment room at the rear, where holistic therapists would offer different services including Indian head massage and reiki sessions. Anita also offered therapies, including shamanic healing and tarot card readings. Ian regularly had a tarot reading with her and would always claim that she was one of the best in this field. As for me, I had a couple of healing sessions with Anita and also attended a number of her Shamanic workshops.

Successively, due to one of Ian's many failed business plans, we left Hampshire to return as a family to our Devon base; this was one of the several occasions that Lauren's schooling was affected by a mix of Ian's pursuit of monetary success and my desire to maintain a family unit. Nonetheless, after our return to Devon, Anita wasn't someone I stayed in contact with on a 1:1 basis; but I did follow her on social media, because of our mutual spiritual interests. After all, the first time I ever met Anita at her shop, she was wearing a pair of angel wings, and this hadn't only made me smile but had made her somewhat unforgettable; never a truer word!

Hence, the Universe had a plan to which I was completely blind but was one which was seemingly hatched as far back as 2013, the year we first met Anita. But little would I realise the full impact of that connection until some 7-10 years later, when we all found ourselves relocating to Spain, to live in the exact same town in the province of Almeria, during COVID and pre-Brexit.

As a result, Anita and consequently, Malcolm, naturally became the closest friends we had in Spain, because we were literally all in the same boat: British ex-pats, striving to make a new life living abroad, arriving during a pandemic. So, it seemed normal that the four of us, would form a friendship. Subsequently, it was also the first time I'd ever seen Ian befriend another male; he usually only had business acquaintances. Nonetheless, Malcolm was an unlikely match for Ian as they were complete opposites; Malcolm liked to talk, wear t-shirts, smoke cigarettes and drink beer. Ian preferred silence, suits, cigars, and coffee.

Through this friendship, it was natural that we would discuss how we managed to fund our lifestyle living abroad, which resulted in Ian telling them all about the trading platform he used. However, Ian felt the need to explain to them about his previously failed business, but the way in which he presented the information made him sound completely blameless.

I believe he did this, not so much to be truthful, but because Anita had previously witnessed our lavish, but fake, Hampshire lifestyle. Therefore, in all likelihood, she was probably wondering why we had ended up with nothing; a scenario that didn't bode well for Ian when attempting to lure them into investing money in the trading scheme.

What was evident is that he truly believed in the trading platform and saw an opportunity to be paid as an introducer to the scheme, which is what he wanted as it would earn him commission. As a result, Malcolm and Anita did become trading clients, which I think is a decision that was made because she had previously known us during Ian's more successful period.

When we met for coffee the day after Ian had the accident, our friends were unsurprisingly curious to find out why my husband was limping and had a bruise to his forehead. Ian complained to them about the incident, sharing with them his thoughts on the need to return to the UK before the poor quality Spanish housing killed him; in addition to the dangerous door, he had a long list of other potential property hazards. Anita listened and offered some caring platitudes, but Malcolm wasn't his usual witty self; he seemed distracted.

After the incident update, Malcolm asked if he could talk to Ian alone. Anita and I were nonplussed at the idea, as it meant that we could have an impromptu girls trip; an idea that appealed to me because I desperately needed time out from Ian.

However, what seemed initially to be a sporadic plan, actually headed me in the direction of what proved to be another major synchronicity. Our spontaneous tour took us to a remote mountain tapas bar that had only recently re-opened after COVID.

We arrived at the bar as first time visitors. We received a warm welcome from the owner, Paco. We ordered food and drinks. When Paco returned with our order, he struck up a friendly conversation and enquired whether we were tourists or locals. I have no idea what prompted me to tell Paco my entire life story, but I ended up sharing with him that I was a local, but not for much longer, if I failed to find a suitable long-term rental property.

Then the miracle happened. Paco smiled and said,

"I think I may be able to help you."

Anita and I went to view the property and I knew instantly that Ian would like the house; it was a remote 3-bed, detached property, set in the mountains; it had a swimming pool, garage, and several terraces with stunning views. Plus, the property was available long-term, and the rent was very reasonable.

The following day, I persuaded Ian to take a look at Paco's property and he liked it enough to consider keeping a rental house in Spain. It wasn't enough for him to completely cancel his plan to return to the UK for business reasons, but it did at least mean that we were not abandoning the idea of a home in Almeria. So, as far as I was concerned, *Casa Serenidad*, was literally, heaven sent.

With the nerves and excitement of presenting the new house to Ian, I forgot for a few days to enquire why Malcolm had wanted to speak to him in private; I wanted to ensure that our friend was okay. However, I wasn't prepared for Ian's response. Malcolm was dying. It turned out that the beer he drank at breakfast, masked as one of the benefits of a retiree's life in the sun, hadn't just started since moving to Spain. He'd been a functioning alcoholic for years and the combination of leaving his job, which helped to form the 'functioning' part, combined with the easy access to cheap booze, had spiralled his condition.

I was further surprised to learn that Anita had known for some time but hadn't really grasped the severity of his drinking problem. Anita had threatened to leave Malcolm on numerous occasions due to his excessive drinking. The issue for her had been his lies, the over-spending and staying out late. What had escaped her, was the seriousness of his condition; the irreparable damage drinking had done to his liver. For both, like many of us, they'd put off dealing with the real issue until tomorrow, when Malcolm was ready to deal with it. But eventually the tomorrows' had run out and within 3-weeks Malcolm was dead.

I grieved for Anita's loss and for the passing of a friend; it wasn't my first experience of death. I understood the consuming pain and vast emptiness of grief; what it was like to have your heart broken in two, to the point that part of you dies too.

But Malcolm's death also made me realise that I wasn't living either; I couldn't remember the last time I'd smiled or laughed. I couldn't recall the last time I'd truly felt seen or heard. I'd forgotten what it was like to be told that I was beautiful, to be kissed, held, or touched. To be made love to. I wondered whether I was still dead inside or whether I was beginning to recognise my own unhappiness in my marriage to Ian.

With my passport still missing, and the move to the new house in progress, Ian decided to delay his trip to the UK. This also allowed us to support Anita in dealing with the aftermath of her loss.

It was at this time another synchronicity came into action.

Ian and I had travelled to Spain to start a new life. The intention was to apply for residential status. Part of this process required us to obtain various revised forms of identification that were recognised in Spain, including the need to surrender our UK driving licence. We had driven to Almeria, travelling via ferry and then by car from northern to southern Spain. Our vehicle, a Range Rover, was registered in the UK in my name. It was necessary, if keeping the UK vehicle in Spain, to have it matriculated: legally registered in the country of residence. There was also a time limit on how soon this process should be actioned.

However, Ian opted to not matriculate the vehicle for various reasons. He was adamant that he would fulfil his billionaire dream and because of this, he believed that one day, he would have his own lavish Hampshire pad. Therefore, his motive for not registering the vehicle in Spain, was that the Range Rover would be his preferred vehicle to use when in the UK; along with the fleet of other prestigious cars, including a Bentley and a Rolls Royce, that he planned to own. He seemed oblivious to the fact that if he ever made that kind of money, he could just buy a new Range Rover.

Nonetheless, his decision to not matriculate the Range Rover, put us at risk of being fined or worse still, having the vehicle seized by the Guardia, because we had exceeded the 90-day rule.

After securing the new rental property, *Casa Serenidad*, which affirmed that Ian was still toying with the idea of living in Spain at least part-time; he decided that he would need a Spanish vehicle for whenever he visited the country. It had proved very expensive to hire a car on a long-term basis: sometimes up to 1000 euros for a month; this was partly the reason why Ian risked driving the Range Rover, but if impounded would far exceed the cost of hiring a car.

He didn't want to risk buying a second hand car due to the language barrier and not knowing anything about mechanics; we could easily have ended up wasting money on an unreliable vehicle. Therefore, his idea was to get a HP car, which we'd learnt about via some other friends from the local village. However, to get a HP car, required a deposit and evidence of monthly earnings, which could include a state pension. However, because we were not homeowners and at the time, not tax resident, we lacked the financial standing normally required for this form of agreement.

In addition to this, there was a shortage of new cars due to the pandemic: factories were closed and the production line for vehicles had stopped. The only cars available was pre-COVID editions, and these were in limited supply. Add to this, Ian's request for an automatic vehicle with a sunshine roof so that he could smoke his cigars and the car salesman was literally in stitches from laughing. He thought that my husband was joking until he realised that he wasn't, and that Ian seriously thought that even after a pandemic he was still entitled to have whatever he wanted. Therefore, the odds were pretty much stacked up against us in our proficiency to have a HP vehicle in Spain.

In reality, none of this would have mattered if I'd been on-board with Ian's plan to return to the UK. The old me, prior to the signs and synchronicities, would have placated Ian with the idea that if we didn't get the car it didn't matter for the time being; it could wait until later. But I was getting increasingly stressed about the outcome of whether we would be able to have HP car.

I think I knew in the back of my mind, that I was not returning to the UK with Ian. I didn't have a plan or even know how or why, that would occur at this point; but internally it became immensely important to me that we got our hands on a vehicle to use in Spain. Our rental property was located on a mountain, which made it vital to have transport. To relocate to an area where we could survive without a car, would mean moving to the coast, which is expensive, and long-term properties are rare.

The car salesman was extremely good at his job. He managed to find a car in Madrid that was automatic but didn't have a sunroof, which as he explained, is not a popular feature with the Spanish who respect the sun and want to avoid its intense heat. He was highly experienced in car sales and knew the system very well. He put Ian's finance application through on a Friday afternoon, when he knew that staff specialising in risk assessment would be either having a siesta or be finished for the weekend. This meant that rather than a real person making the decision as to whether the HP car finance would be granted, the computer made a decision, and the salesman knew how to give the latter the data it required to secure a positive outcome.

As a result, the finance was granted and Ian became the main registered contract holder for a wonderful new blue Ford; it had to be Ian's name on the agreement, as it was his UK state pension that secured the deal. Notably, the car registration included, 888.

Meanwhile, I was still suffering with pain in my feet. Likewise, Ian wasn't recovering from his fall: his hip was bad, and he was still limping with pain; I hated to see him in any discomfort. He'd refused to get a check-up after the fall, as he didn't want to waste his medical insurance on something that would heal in time. So, I took it upon myself to try and find someone who could help Ian privately, without the use of his medical policy.

Some years previously, I'd devised my own unique method for sourcing a therapist to help me manage my panic attacks. I hadn't wanted to go to my GP as I didn't want my anxiety to be recorded on my medical records and it would always be my preference to find an alternative solution to mainstream medication if possible.

Using guidance, I had sourced an amazing hypnotherapist called Paula, via the Yellow Pages. During my initial appointment, she asked me why I'd chosen her from a long list of other local practitioners. I didn't want to tell her that I'd been guided to her, so I lied, and said the first thing that came into my mind: I told her that I'd selected her because she was the first female listed. She sounded somewhat surprised and said,

"Well, that's interesting... because the angels told me that you were coming."

Paula turned out to be the perfect practitioner for me, and therefore, I used the same system to find someone who could help Ian. The only difference was that we were living abroad, and the Yellow Pages no longer existed. Therefore, I was guided to search the Internet for 'physiotherapy' and 'massage' therapists in Almeria, and once a directory of suggested practitioners was provided, I was guided to choose the 11th person on the list.

The 11th person on the list was named, Manuel Angel.

I laughed when I saw both names. Angel is a common name for men in Spain and is pronounced as An-kel. A man with the middle name of Angel was enough to put a smile on my face. Additionally, I'd learnt from my interest in the angelic realms that notably, many of the archangel names end with the letters e-l, i.e., Micha-el, Rapha-el and Gabri-el, which I understood to mean 'of God'.

Manu-el Ank-el!?

I liked the name and so via email, I booked an appointment for Ian. He was reluctant to go at first; he was insistent that he would wait to see a 'professional' in the UK. However, with my passport still missing Ian wasn't sure how long he would have to wait until he could seek the preferred medical attention; even he recognised that an indefinite pain from an injury wasn't a viable or comfortable option.

I went with Ian for his first appointment. Outside Manuel Angel's practice, a laminated sign printed in Spanish and English advised patients to ring the doorbell and to wait until the door opened. Ian rang the bell and we waited.

Just above the doorbell I noticed a plaque embedded within the stone wall that depicted an image of Jesus surrounded in a golden haze. My family hadn't been religious, but my mum had suffered from mental ill health, which had created a childhood that had felt unsafe and volatile.

I'd never read the Bible but had found images of Jesus in a children's edition strangely comforting. He became my imaginary friend, who whenever I was scared, I would talk to Him and imagine that he was at my side. I'd long forgotten this feeling and recalling it felt like home, like a piece of me had been restored.

Eventually, a buzzer denoted that the door was unleashed, which was our cue to enter the building. Ian was greeted by a man who I rightly assumed was Manuel.

"You must be Ian?"

Ian and Manuel shook hands. Manuel looked in my direction and awaited for an introduction.

"Oh, this is my wife, Eva"

Did he just call me Eva? What if it was the bump to his head?

Ian had never actually married his late partner Eva but would insist on always referring to her as his 'late wife'.

"Actually, my name is Chloe…"

Ian shot a disapproving glance at me; how dare I correct him? I guessed nothing had changed, that the bump hadn't impaired years of repetitive behaviour. Manuel smiled.

"Chloe, that's a beautiful name."

I was instantly captivated: a combination of Manuel's gentle brown eyes and all-round energy, plus the way his Spanish accent pronounced my name, making it sound exotic and interesting, rendered me spellbound.

He shook my hand too and the handhold seemed to linger. It wasn't inappropriate but felt as if he was reading my energy. Oddly, Manuel's touch felt familiar: I found myself thinking about Jesus and remembering how as a friend he had brought me comfort in childhood. I got lost in my thoughts, to the point of momentarily losing track of time.

When I returned to the moment, I felt intense embarrassment, because I was concerned that I'd equally allowed myself to linger for too long in the warm greeting. Whenever I felt self-conscious, I would consider what the other person saw in me; in Manuel Angel's case, I decided that he would see a crazy, middle-aged woman overwhelmed by simple warm kindness.

Ian coughed, which was an indication that my behaviour displeased him. I noted the look in his face, which confirmed my notion.

I was guided to a waiting room before Ian disappeared with Manuel for treatment. As I took a seat, my face was still flushed with embarrassment and at the same time, I could feel fear churning in my stomach: I was worried that my behaviour had irritated Ian. I was also concerned that if Manuel Angel was unable to help Ian, that he would be really annoyed if the visit proved to be a waste of time and money.

I began to feel nauseous. I hated confrontation as much as I disliked Ian's silent treatment; both felt equally ominous. Feeling stressed, I buried my head in my hands. Moments later, I heard the waiting room door click open: I looked up expecting to see the next client but instead saw Manuel.

He looked at me so intently that I felt like he was staring right into my soul; it was the kind of look I associated with unconditional love. A gaze I'd rarely seen from others and only in the presence of truly like-minded spiritual souls. It said *I see you;* I didn't know what to do or say. My emotions felt erratic; I felt awkward and yet safe. I wanted to collapse in a heap and to cry as if tomorrow would never come. Before I could say or do anything, I watched as he took a seat on the floor in front of me.

Manuel told me that Ian was fine and that he'd left him for ten minutes under a heat lamp. In the meantime, he wanted to find out what was wrong with my feet and as he asked the question, he reached out to touch them. I'm not entirely sure what initially caused me to recoil: whether it was the idea that I didn't want to be touched or what felt like an electric shock when his fingers brushed my toes, that made me pull back. Whichever it was, I know that I definitely felt stupid for flinching and as usual, my embarrassment caused me to look down at the eczema on my hands; they looked old beyond their years. I felt small. I wanted the ground to open and swallow me up.

"I won't hurt you Chloe…"

I avoided looking at Manuel for what felt like ages. I tried to think of something to say, but words failed me. Eventually, in the calm silence, I dared to look at him and saw only a face that spoke of gentleness, and I knew instantly, that he wasn't only telling me the truth, but that I was also meant to meet him. I can only describe this moment as a 'deep knowing', an unfathomable feeling that struck a chord that resonated with my core. He held his hand open so that I could take hold of it. As the palm of my hand tentatively lowered toward his, I could feel a shaft of energy emanating from his hand. Confused, I paused and sat with my hand hovering over his. He gently said to me,

"I feel it too."

I wasn't sure what we were feeling, what label to give to it; but I suddenly felt like I had known him forever. The same voice that spoke to me in the early hours of the morning to tell me to look at the clock whispered,

"He's healed you before and you've healed him."

I had a vision of an ancient temple, a sensation of Goddess figures and hands radiating with healing energy. In my mind, I gazed up to look at the owner of the hands to see a male figure, which felt like he had Christ energy. It felt like the same force I could feel from Manuel. I didn't believe that Manuel Angel was Jesus, but I certainly felt that he worked on his energetic ray. In my soul, Manuel Angel, felt like home, for me, he was a real life angel.

This beautiful soul was able to help Ian but also advised him that I urgently needed to tend to the issue in my feet. If it was left unattended, it would get worse, and Manuel Angel advised that this wouldn't be of benefit to either of us.

He spoke to Ian in a way that felt like he knew that he would have to put a strong and persuasive case forward to enable me to have treatment. Intuitively, he seemed to know that it was important to highlight the disadvantage it would cause Ian if I wasn't fully functioning.

Manuel Angel recommended that I would need at least four sessions before he could assess how well I was responding to treatment.

On the drive back home with Ian, I was thankful that he'd found the appointment with Manuel Angel beneficial. However, he didn't book a follow-up session because his mindset was that the treatment would tie him over until he got back to the UK. This meant that he didn't see himself as returning to Manuel Angel's practice, which without Ian, I would not be able to attend myself.

I tentatively tried to discuss my feet issue, but Ian offered no sympathy toward me for the extreme pain I was experiencing. Instead, he presented the all too familiar caustic jokes about needing a younger model as I was no longer fit for purpose. He used the same level of so-called humour to tell me that I was falling apart; he claimed that I always had something wrong with me. This wasn't true; the only time I had something wrong with me is when the issue didn't get addressed. His comments hurt, but it was pointless telling him how I felt because he would tell me that he was joking and that I was too sensitive or lacked a sense of fun.

The rest of the journey home was done in silence. But I felt like I'd had my eyes opened; that I was supposed to meet Manual Angel, so that I could experience what genuine care, warmth and unconditional love felt like. I was so used to normalising Ian's behaviour that I needed to learn what was missing in my life and to recognise that I deserved to be treated better.

From that day onwards, the day that I met Manuel Angel, it was the beginning of the point of no return. It was as if I simply surrendered to what would be: stopped trying to struggle to row upstream but allowed myself to go with the flow. Once I did that, my life with Ian began to unravel at a profound speed.

Days later, Ian announced his imminent return to the UK on his own; he stated that he wasn't willing to hang around waiting for me. He claimed that I could join him as soon as I received my passport.

He opted to drive to Bilbao, where he planned to catch the overnight ferry back to Portsmouth. Taking the Range Rover would enable Ian to pack extra clothing as he was uncertain how long he would be gone. My initial reaction was to wonder how I was going to manage driving after 12 years; the mountain roads were scary. Ian told me that he was done with hanging around for the purpose of being my taxi driver.

Ian drove me to one more session with Manuel Angel before eventually departing to the UK. During my session with Manuel Angel, I didn't want to talk. I just wanted to feel well and for the pain to stop in my feet. Manuel Angel worked in silence; he massaged my feet and calves. Eventually, he said to me that he felt that my pain was a manifestation of emotional trauma. The example he gave was, sexual abuse.

Ian left for the UK the day before my 50th birthday. It had been some time since he'd last bought me a gift; as far as he was concerned, it had become an unnecessary cost. However, before he departed, he offered me a package containing a beautiful candle and a mug with the image of Frida Kahlo; oddly the first gifts he'd given me that felt deeply personal as if he did know me well after all.

Anita wasn't going to allow me to spend my big birthday on my own. She knew that I didn't want to drive the HP car, so she collected me from home. She cooked a Sunday roast lunch, on a hot Andalusian sunny day, for a bunch of her fellow golfers who were all strangers to me. Lunch turned into a party of endless food, drink, banter, and loud music; everything I could have wanted but somehow had been denied over the years. And yet, with such effort made to create the perfect birthday celebration, I felt alone. I also felt confused. I hadn't wanted to return to the UK with Ian, and yet his departure made me feel discarded and abandoned. Then doubt set in, which prompted the belief that I couldn't survive without him, and this terrified me.

I was stood alone with an empty wine glass, watching everyone else enjoy my birthday party, when a guy, who I later learnt was called Roy approached me. He offered to top up my glass and at the same time struck up a conversation.

He told me that Anita had mentioned to him that I may need his help. He explained how in the UK his profession had been a driving instructor and that he understood that I needed to get back on the road.

There was no way that the angels or Source, was going to allow me to give up.

The next day, two days after Ian's departure, I was informed that my passport had finally arrived. The day after that, Roy took me for a driving lesson in the HP vehicle. Roy was accustomed to helping drivers rebuild their confidence. My first destination was to see if I could drive to Manuel Angel's practice. After a few driving lessons, I began to drive on my own for the first time in over a decade.

The more I drove the more chores I was able to complete on my own. I loved the independence and freedom that driving permitted me. I was still nervous, and I had to adapt my routes on a daily basis, because there were roads or junctions that felt unsafe. However, Roy had encouraged me to just keep driving and even if I had to do a 10km detour, that it was more important to keep practicing than to stop again.

Everyday chores such as visiting the bank or the currency exchange, were challenging, but gave me such a sense of achievement when completed. I enjoyed going to the petrol station, supermarket, and coffee shops; I even got used to driving up a mountain road to drop the rental fee with Paco. Everywhere I went, were all places that I used to visit with Ian, therefore, everyone was used to seeing us together.

However, in Ian's absence, these virtual strangers working on checkouts, as bank cashiers and garage forecourt attendants, began to comment on how well I looked. I would be asked what I'd done to appear much brighter and confident. A woman in the currency exchange jokingly suggested to a colleague that my sunnier disposition was because I'd ditched my husband. Elsewhere, a coffee shop waiter commented that being alone suited me; he said that I'd come out of the shadows.

Ian would call me every day from the UK, notably, he never asked me whether I was okay. He never enquired about my driving or checked to see if there was anything I needed, especially living alone. Instead, he complained of microwave dinners and un-ironed shirts; implying that my absence had left him fending for himself. Aware that my passport had arrived, Ian's main concern was to establish how soon did I plan to join him. Each time he enquired about my travel arrangements; my stomach would churn with fear. I would avoid committing to answering the question and offer some excuse that I needed to continue having treatment on my feet.

I shared my thoughts regarding Ian not only with Anita but two of my UK girlfriends, Niks and Hazel. I was stunned to learn that both of them had a deep dislike of him. The first claimed that she'd always felt that Ian had tried to discourage our friendship as a means to keeping me to himself. Hazel stated that he'd taken her aside on several occasions to talk about his concerns regarding my psychological well-being; he'd told her that I suffered from severe black dog moods. He'd implied to her that I was unstable and because of this, she should never mention his conversation with her to me, as this could push me over the edge. Both advised that I should leave Ian.

I was deeply upset that my friends had chosen to not talk to me about their concerns regarding Ian or myself. However, I can understand that they felt that I'd already been through enough relationship hardships; one divorce and the death of a partner, leaving me on both occasions, a lone parent to my daughter, Lauren. Nonetheless, the girls' advice to leave Ian wasn't something that I took lightly. I needed more than just the advice of loyal girlfriends who would always choose to side with me regardless of whether my own thoughts or actions were justified.

Therefore, I made the decision to call Walt. He was an old and trusted professional friend. I met him during my years working in broadcast media. I'd worked behind the scenes in news and Walt was a police contact, who would be invited to comment on issues relating to domestic violence. I felt that Walt would offer me a professional, unbiased, male, viewpoint on my situation; and that is what he gave me.

"In my opinion Chloe, you have been a victim of domestic abuse for twenty years: systematic psychological abuse, at the hands of a narcissist. You are the perfect candidate for people like him. If I was talking to you at the station, I'd be suggesting you move to a safe house. But as that isn't an option, I'm advising you to get out, while you still can; it will only get worse."

Walt had continued to advise that I return to the UK to live with a friend where I could much more easily seek the support I needed, both legal and from organisations offering support to victims of domestic violence. While a return to the UK would have been the easier option, I simply knew that regardless of the language barrier, my age, lack of money and employment options, that I had to stay in Spain.

As a result, Walt was only able to continue supporting me as a friend. He advised that I seek out comparable organisations in Spain that could help me through the process of dealing with long term domestic abuse. Thus, using the same method that I used to find Manuel Angel, I found a lawyer named, Fernando.

I was overwhelmed by Fernando's belief in me. I didn't have to justify my need for assistance, provide evidence and lists with dates and times of abusive incidents. He simply believed me and when I asked why he did, he told me that he'd been doing his job long enough to recognise the fear in abuse victims.

Fernando's priority was to find me the support and advice I needed to help me recognise and heal from 20-years of abuse. To this day, Fernando has never charged me for the time and dedication he gave to helping me. In those early fearful days, he became a voice in a country where I was the foreigner and unable to communicate. Whenever we met, he bought my coffees and breakfast because he knew that I had limited resources.

Through Fernando, I was earmarked for a series of 1:1 sessions via the Spanish equivalent of the domestic violence unit (DVU). I was allocated a psychotherapist called Maria, who specialised in narcissistic abuse. I was also allocated an interpreter.

Maria's role was to help me recognise the red flags of narcissistic abuse. Her approach was gentle, but it left no stone unturned, as every notable aspect of my life with Ian, became examples of typical abuse tactics. What astonished me was that I didn't have to justify how I felt or give examples of events that had created the uneasy doubtful niggle I was experiencing. Instead, it was a process that was carefully designed to ask relevant questions so as to ease the information out of me rather than place me on the spot to narrate instances.

Nonetheless, my life soon began to read like a list of tick box events, used by the narcissist. Find a vulnerable person who preferably has no family ties (tick). Make them feel special and loved beyond their wildest dreams (tick). Lure them into a sense of safety so that they share their most intimate fears and dreams with you; make note of these and use at a later date when you need something from them (tick). Be quick to commit to a long-term relationship, this will add to their sense of feeling loved (tick). Offer them the dream life but ensure that this means they move away from existing family, friends, home, and career if applicable. Ultimately isolate them (tick). As soon as they have relocated to share your life and there is no possibility of them returning back home, fuck with their head (tick).

Ultimately, Maria's professional assessment of my relationship with Ian was textbook narcissistic. Twenty years of cruelly calculated manipulation and control, with extensive psychological abuse that played upon my deep rooted fears. The hardest part was being told that a narcissist isn't capable of real love or affection, which meant that any love I'd experienced, hadn't been real on his part. Thus, once more, the professional advice was to prioritise my safety and mental well-being.

I cannot profess that my experience makes me an expert in narcissistic abuse. However, two years on from taking the leap of faith, I think it's important to remember that many of the 'red flags' associated with narcissistic abuse can be innocently evident in other individuals.

To be quickly showered with love and affection in the early stages of a relationship, for example, doesn't automatically make the 'offender' a narcissist. Likewise, as advised by my psychotherapist Maria, many of the traits are often recognised within different generations and cultures, but again, this doesn't create a narcissist. Therefore, I use this label with care and respect for every person who has been victim to this hideous and often hidden form of silent abuse.

Notably, while it was my spiritual faith that helped me to recognise that not all was well in my marriage, I cannot stress enough, that having a belief, other in yourself, is a necessary prerequisite to going on your own journey. It is important that anyone who feels that they are a victim of abuse reach out to friends or professionals. You aren't wasting anyone's time. Help is available. Nothing that you will say will shock or be judged. Seeking advice is highly confidential. Please also remember that abuse doesn't always have to be physical; it can be silent too. Trust your instinct, your gut feeling to always know what is best for you. Feel it. Own it. No one has the right to take this from you. For me, it took 20-years to recognise that I was being abused; I lost two decades of my life.

This is my story. It may not suit everyone, but I hope it serves a purpose for some in bringing Light and comfort in knowing that you aren't walking this path alone.

"Let's just make it easy: narcissist, sociopath, psychopath, no need to distinguish which is which. They all simply suffer from person syndrome. Avoidance is the only known treatment. Don't set yourself on fire to keep someone else warm."

[Source: Unknown]

1

THE FIRST 20 YEARS

Red Flags: Love Bombing / Quick to Commit

Twenty years ago, I hadn't heard of the term 'love-bombing' but now, most people have heard this phrase and quite often like the word 'narcissist', in my humble opinion, are words that are used too flippantly to complain about another person. If we aren't careful about what words we use when referencing someone, to the point that it becomes too casual and mainstream, we devalue the seriousness of the subject that the word is intended to describe. This can mean that when someone finds the courage to talk about abuse that they may not be heard, because the description of the experience has become too generic.

Love-bombing is usually the first phase of narcissistic abuse. The narcissist will shower the partner with an overwhelming amount of affection, compliments, and attention. They will literally sweep them off their feet with grand romantic gestures, buying lavish gifts, excessive communication and making plans for the future, all of which, makes their victim feel special.

The goal of love-bombing is to create a deep sense of connection and dependency, which makes the partner more vulnerable to the narcissist's manipulation and control tactics as the relationship progresses. The narcissist is often extremely charming, which can make it very difficult to recognise the manipulative nature of their behaviour.

Nonetheless, I needed the professional help of Maria, the Spanish based psychotherapist, to point it out to me that I'd been love-bombed by Ian. In hindsight, it seems so very obvious, but at the time of the experience, I truly believed that he'd fallen head over heels in love with me: I wanted to believe that people could fall in love at first sight.

In 2000, I was a single mum. I'd only ever had two romantic relationships: the first had been with Mac, who was the father of my daughter, Lauren. However, as soon as I became a mum, Mac had an affair with a colleague, Dee, and our marriage ended in divorce. I then met Hugh and he was an amazing man who I believed I would be with for the rest of my life; he was also a magnificent father figure to Lauren. I truly believed that Hugh was my soulmate. But Hugh died at the age of 45 from cardiomyopathy; his heart literally just stopped working.

His death occurred on the eve of Halloween, it was all very dark and bleak, the stuff of nightmares. I'd taken Lauren out for 'trick or treat', helped her gather a bucket load of sweets and handed out treats to the neighbourhood children. After I'd bathed Lauren and tucked her up in bed with a magical story; something lighter for Halloween, I snuggled down to watch a horror movie on TV; Hugh was working late.

I don't recall Hugh coming to bed. I was awoken by his snoring in the early hours of the following morning. I gently nudged him in the hope that it would prompt him to stop breathing heavily, but the deep guttural sound continued. Not wishing to wake him, I then carefully attempted to turn him onto his side, but he felt heavier than normal and suddenly, something didn't feel right.

I dived out of bed and turned on the light. I tried desperately to wake Hugh up but failed. I raced downstairs and called the emergency services; I made the call on a static landline phone. I had to run back and forth, up and down the stairs, to carry out what the emergency services advisor instructed me to do. I was convinced that Hugh was still alive; I could feel a heartbeat and believed that he could be saved. However, in the midst of the terrifying drama, I'd mistaken my own wild heartbeat as his pulse; I couldn't decipher where the boundaries of our life force energies began and ended. He was gentle and kind. It was easy to get lost in him.

The police routinely attended the sudden death scenario due to Hugh's age. The police officer advised me to not avoid telling my daughter the truth regarding her stepfather's death; delaying the truth would make it harder to heal long term. However, explaining to a four-year-old that her stepfather wasn't ever going to come home again was difficult. Even so, I followed the officer's advice and told Lauren the truth and naturally she was deeply affected by the loss.

When someone dies it is difficult to avoid evaluating spiritual beliefs, especially when it was a discussion that Hugh and I never shared; we didn't think we needed to. I found myself having to second-guess what his death wishes would be, while at the same time, feeling nothing but anger. I had my own unspoken belief system that involved acknowledging that there was something greater than myself, but it was an idea that I refused to label, as my thoughts on the subject weren't fully formed enough to know what hashtag summed up my faith.

Likewise, my belief system hadn't really progressed much beyond my childhood years when I imagined Jesus to be a fictional friend and God as an entity to be feared. I'd considered the notion that befriending Jesus had been a childhood coping mechanism; a friend who I'd subconsciously ditched as soon as I left home.

Nonetheless, considering that I didn't have a title to give my belief system, my faith was still deep enough for me to feel SO ANGRY at my version of God for allowing us, especially my daughter, to have witnessed her birth father run off with another woman and then her second father figure die. I thought I was too young to experience both, but she was just four-years-old.

As a result, Hugh's death felt deeply personal, as though we were being singled out by this uncertain God entity. I couldn't understand why bad things always seemed to happen to me. It felt as though I wasn't allowed to be happy; that as soon as I felt any sense of joy, such as, fall in love, that it would be taken away.

My workplace granted time off work and I was inundated with condolence cards and flowers. The cards often spoke of God and faith and being held by Him, but I didn't feel that way; I felt as though He had abandoned us. I swore to Him that I would never ever forgive Him for what he'd done to us; I vowed that I would never speak God's name again.

Amongst the influx of cards was several small angelic gifts in the form of figurines or angel wings. At first, they were among the initial condolence cards and gifts. I immediately liked them because they felt separate from God but still instilled a sense of comfort. However, when Hugh's death became yesterday's news, angelic gifts would randomly continue to arrive at my home. A close friend or work colleague would see an angelic statuette or card or fridge magnet with some angelic words of wisdom printed upon it. The item would make them think of me and the gift would be bought and sent.

I appreciated every single angelic gift, not just because of the heavenly iconic image, but also due to the gifts being sent by colleagues who weren't close friends, but people who had wanted to show their support in the only way they knew how. Likewise, I would be sent similar gifts from distant friends of Hugh, people who I met for the first time at his funeral. Yet somehow, everyone was tuning into the fact that angels would bring comfort to both Lauren and me. The timing of their arrival would be always when I needed them the most. I would be trying my hardest to hold life together; portraying myself as a pillar of strength in front of Lauren, while hiding the worse pain I'd ever experienced, which was grief.

Therefore, when I say that angels brought me comfort it was instinctive, part of my internal being, that recognised that the angelic symbol brought inner peace. I don't doubt that culturally they are routinely in our subconscious, even when born into a non-religious family: I still attended school assembly, played a shepherd in a nativity play and we celebrated Christmas which would have encouraged iconic images of Jesus in the manger, the Wise Men, the Star of Bethlehem, and angels. I guess what these occasions do, especially when your childhood is volatile, is create a place that feels safe. You don't need to understand it or to be able to quote passages from Bible text, but something is stirred within the heart centre that feels like home. And that is what the angels felt like, they felt like home.

I also recall my paternal grandma, Theresa, speaking only once about the death of her brother during the Second World War. She told me that his spirit had visited her at night, and she knew instantly that he had died. She spoke of a poem that had been said to her as a child. It was a poem about four angels at your bed.

I believe it was this poem:

> *Matthew, Mark, Luke, and John,*
> *Bless the bed that I lie on.*
> *Four corners to my bed,*
> *Four angels round my head.*
> *One to watch and one to pray*
> *And two to bear the soul away.*
>
> [Source: Unknown/various adaptations]

The thought that my non-religious grandma chose to believe that the angels gently carried her brother's soul away to bring comfort, felt like an important and timely memory. It felt like she'd passed on a message that was always given with the intention that one day I would need to refer to it. I loved my Grandma Theresa, and therefore, in my time of need, to think of her and to feel that somehow, she'd wanted me to remember this story brought me solace. The news of her brother's death had arrived the following day.

After Hugh's sudden death, Lauren started having difficulties with sleeping. Likewise, during the day, her schoolteacher or childminder couldn't leave her side, without tantrums and screaming sessions. The poor little thing was clearly traumatised and fearful that people would continue to disappear from her life. Mac experienced the same when she visited him; except he had a double dose as she would be terrified that she would lose both of her parents. We didn't know what to do to help her as she still seemed too young to be able to put into words what she was feeling.

One day, my friend Hazel took me out for lunch to a large shopping precinct. I wasn't in the mood to buy clothes and my restless nights gave me a permanent headache, which felt worse beneath the artificial mall lighting. We chose to eat at a popular chain restaurant, which allowed us to sit on a pretty terrace overlooking the precinct; everywhere was buzzing and big TV screens blasted out commercials and music. My emotions were extremely raw, I was worried about Lauren and my job; so, the surrounding noise was overwhelming. I excused myself claiming that I needed to nip to the bathroom; en-route I walked past a bookstore and in the window was a book about using angels to help children deal with grief. I bought the book.

At bedtime, the idea was for the parent to read a story about the *Rainbow Bridge* and during the tale, encourage the child to visualise that they were on the bridge, which was surrounded by angels. The bridge linked this world to the other side, where lost loved ones go to live in a place that is beautiful and makes them happy. Each night I used the story to help Lauren to imagine herself walking across the *Rainbow Bridge* holding the hand of an angel. On the other side of the bridge, she could speak to Hugh and tell him about her day and ask about his.

I would encourage her to think about what he would be doing in this perfect place; she would imagine him fishing and catching trout and cooking it for the two of them for dinner. She would also see him singing a song to her while playing his guitar; these were the special moments that they used to share.

Although I'd acknowledged the police officer's advice to tell Lauren the truth regarding Hugh's death, I had no idea how far 'truth' needed to go and by whose definition is the actual truth in this scenario defined. Thus naturally, I questioned whether angels and the *Rainbow Bridge* method was an untruth that encouraged her to hold onto Hugh's memory. But she was four-years-old, and using angels to help her deal with loss, clearly brought her solace, and it helped her to sleep and to speak about Hugh with fondness rather than sadness.

Nevertheless, experiencing death wasn't all fluffy angels. I still had to deal with the trauma of waking up next to Hugh's dead body. Memories of the 999 call, an operator asking me if I could feel a pulse, the fear and confusion, following resuscitation instructions, which involved inserting my fingers into Hugh's throat, only to discover that his airways were blocked with food.

I recall the sound of my anguished cry on realising that he was already dead. It was a sound that didn't feel like it came from me, not from my mouth, but from my soul. I sounded like a pained animal; a noise that is universally understood without the need of explanation. It felt primal and raw, allowed me to know myself on a different level. It also turned my entire life not only upside down, but inside out, quashed, ravaged, and ripped it to shreds, leaving me raw and empty. All of which, further fuelled my anger with God.

In this anguished state, death felt like an actual presence, an energy that lingered for days after Hugh's passing. It felt as though a large dark ominous cloud of energy had gathered across the house, that almost pulsated with a high vibrational hum. It was so strong I would scream at it to take me too; I didn't fear it, I just challenged it. My thought wasn't to leave Lauren behind, it was just my anger and my way of sticking two-fingers up at God because He had taken everything from us. He had taken my first real experience of love; Hugh was my soulmate and father figure to my daughter. I was grieving, we both were. Yet beneath the surface of my pain and anger, I was unaware that my future journey had already been written in the stars

Hugh died seven weeks before our planned wedding date. As a result, I not only had to organise a funeral, but I also had to cancel a wedding at the same time. This created a series of painful conversations and the realisation that not everyone is supportive and understanding. It felt like I had to fight for everything. Hugh had taken early retirement from the police force to pursue his passion for music; he was the lead singer in a band, and also performed solo and in a duo with myself. However, the income stream suddenly stopped, but the wedding venue wouldn't consider a refund; there was pressure to return Hugh's monthly police pension, which was paid in advance and even his agent, while expressing their condolences wanted commission payments for music gigs they had organised for Hugh's band.

Hugh was a gifted blues singer; he was singing the blues the night he died. Everyone wanted a piece of what was left even to the point that while he was still in the chapel of rest there was requests for his band equipment, specifically his guitar and PA system. I was still trying to decide whether I should bury him wearing a suit or stage outfit and the wedding ring I'd bought for him; I couldn't think of anything else. I said no to the requests, I needed time, and this was met with disapproval by his immediate family, agent, and band members.

Thus, an already painfully dark period of my life was escalated daily via the sometimes rightful or thoughtless actions of others. Before I knew it, weeks had passed and the day we should have got married arrived. Lauren went to stay with her birth father Mac, leaving me in the company of my then friend and neighbour, Sandy.

Sandy wanted to take my mind off what should have been my wedding day. I was invited to spend 24 hours with her and her boyfriend Luke. They cooked me a Sunday roast dinner, plied me with alcohol, including an entire bottle of brandy, which I accepted regardless of the fact that I hardly ever drank. I was introduced to another first, smoking weed, never to be repeated. Regardless, it all felt like a total waste of time as nothing could ease the intense grief that I was experiencing.

It was impossible to prevent my mind from picturing Hugh and I exchanging vows and Lauren as our bridesmaid, presenting us our silver Celtic wedding bands. We had invited 22 guests and the plan was for Hugh to perform with his band. The band would continue playing while we danced. I imagined that Lauren would dance with us, making us into three; her resting her feet on ours, moving awkwardly but together as a self-made family unit.

No amount of food, booze or weed was ever going to erase thoughts of what should have been.

While my mood sank, Sandy took it upon herself to find me a new man; she wanted to help me be happy again. She went online to a dating site to find someone suitable. I wasn't interested, I just wanted to be with Hugh. It was the early days of online dating, and the site entries were listed more like a newspaper small-ad with no photograph and limited words.

Among hundreds of less suitable ads, Sandy came across one that she claimed sounded perfect for me. The guy in question was quoting poetry, something about a knight in shining armour seeking to rescue a princess. I was totally disinterested, but she still continued to respond on my behalf and basically, this is how I met Ian. Other friends had said at the time that it was a good omen that a friend, Sandy, had been responsible for introducing me to Ian. Seemingly even back then, there was a belief that it was fate that we should be together.

I have no idea what Sandy put in the initial contact email, in response to his ad. I didn't think to ask. Online dating was a relatively new concept; therefore, I had no preconceived ideas as to whether it was a good way to meet someone. It never crossed my mind that it could be unsafe to share personal details. Plus, I was really not interested in meeting anyone, so I had already decided that I could ignore messages if I needed to.

I don't know how quickly Ian and I got into telling each other our life stories. I don't know who shared the most first. What I do know is that Ian was twenty years older than me, and we seemed to have a lot in common. We had both married our first ever boy or girlfriend; the marriages had ended when our spouses had an affair. We both had children from the marriage. In my case, I had Lauren with Mac and for Ian, he had a son and daughter, Ollie, and Olivia, with his ex-wife Jane. We had both then met someone else believing we had found a forever true love, and yet, both our previous partners had died.

The only difference was that Hugh died suddenly from cardiomyopathy, whereas Eva had died from cancer; for Ian he had witnessed her slow demise. He spoke of taking her on drives across Dartmoor and Exmoor for her to see the landscape, never knowing whether it would be the last time, until it was. He portrayed himself as a man who had cared for a woman very deeply. They hadn't been together that long when she had been diagnosed with terminal cancer. Her home and family lived in Paris and yet she stayed in the UK with Ian, where he claimed to have nursed her. This made him sound empathetic, gentle, and loving, which were traits, after what I'd experienced, I found attractive. Sudden death had been a terribly traumatic experience and yet, I admired Ian's strength to support and love Eva knowing that the person he loved was dying.

Therefore, our initial emails were very deep and intense, open, and honest. We both seemed to understand one another, and our grief allowed us to accept that for a time, there would be four of us in the relationship.

We eventually exchanged photographs. Ian was extremely handsome; my first reaction was that I wouldn't be his type. I sent a dated picture of me, some years younger. I hadn't tried to deliberately deceive Ian, I felt that the photo I'd sent was a good representation of me. I hadn't changed much and was in fact, much slimmer due to grief and stress compared to the version of me in the outdated photo.

My reason for not sending a more recent picture of myself, was mainly due to my hair. Hugh had loved my hair, which was normally shoulder-length, thick blonde curls. However, the stress caused by his death had affected my entire body. My skin was dry and had a greyish appearance, my hair was thinning, the curls had gone, and I was left with a frizzy dry mess. I did not want to share this version of me with anyone. I hoped that it would be temporary.

Ian and I, communicated by email for a week or so, and then advanced to phone calls. Ian seemed very well spoken and at times, struggled to understand my Yorkshire accent. I learnt that he ran a business with his brother Paul, he was Head of Sales, which involved him travelling all over the UK. His home base was in Devon, but he lived most of his time out of a suitcase due to the nature of his business.

After Hugh's death, I eventually returned to my work in media; I worked in TV production in Leeds. I worked shifts, which soon proved to be challenging as a single parent. However, I was fortunate to meet a parent at Lauren's playschool who due to her recent divorce was looking for an additional income stream. She offered to help with Lauren's childcare and was happy to be flexible to fit around my irregular 24/7 work patterns.

One day, while I was at work, I received a text from Ian saying that he was travelling via Leeds and that on the off-chance that I was available, he wanted to invite me for afternoon tea at a local hotel. My initial reaction was one of horror because I wasn't dressed for a date and my hair still resembled candy floss. I was wearing a hideous floral skirt and pink jumper; it was my attempt to appear bright and happy, but my true intention was to spend most of the day hiding in my office programme planning and drinking coffee.

Thus ideally, I wanted to turn down the invite as I didn't like to be surprised; I at least, would have liked to have looked my best. However, we did have a lot in common and I was concerned that if I said no to the invite, that I wouldn't be given a second chance to meet him. So, I agreed to afternoon tea, which I admit, I didn't know then, what that consisted; I expected something along the lines of a simple cup of tea.

Therefore, the first time that I met Ian was while I was at work. I offered him a tour of the studios and spoke with pride about my job; I had worked hard to gain a career in media, working my way up from news-desk secretary to studio director. However, Ian was disinterested from the offset. I initially put this down to nerves and him being on a tight schedule. So, I kept the tour and talk short and allowed him to whisk me off in his Mercedes Estate to the Grand Hotel in Leeds, for afternoon tea.

Once we'd arrived at the hotel, it was easier to get an impression of Ian. The date felt somewhat formal, as he didn't attempt polite small talk, such as general niceties or compliments; this made the occasion lack warmth. However, he was well presented and spoken. He had this air about him that suggested that he was used to the finer things in life.

It was evident to Ian that the afternoon tea came as a huge surprise to me; I was flabbergasted by the quantity and selection of sandwiches and cakes. I was also a little overwhelmed by the hotel's afternoon tea ambiance; guests were extremely well dressed and some of the women were wearing hats. I felt uncomfortable and out of place, which made me highly nervous. I felt overwhelmed making a simple decision as to whether I liked milk or lemon with my tea; it felt like a trick question and one that I was bound to get wrong.

As if sensing my unease, Ian began to explain the ritual of partaking in afternoon tea; I learnt of the importance of drinking tea from fine bone china, the correct etiquette of selecting sandwiches and cakes, and how to use a fine cotton napkin. The need to have a lesson in etiquette felt humiliating, regardless of whether it was given with good intent. Just as my face was flushing with shame, Ian leant forward to wipe crumbs from my lips: I felt uncertain as to whether this added further awkwardness to the situation or if it was a sign of affection.

Almost as soon as our date had started, Ian began to talk about his late partner, Eva. While he spoke, he excused himself from joining me for afternoon tea; he told me to help myself. After his lesson on decorum, it seemed a little off that he would then claim that he preferred to drink coffee and that he didn't want to eat; he advised me that both he and Eva had always limited their intake of carbs as it was their wish to stay in shape. He shared photographs of Eva with me; she certainly was very beautiful.

I continued to listen to tales regarding Eva's beauty as I politely ate the afternoon tea, while pondering why he would order something that was so clearly laden with the offending carbs. I wasn't sure what was the customary amount of sandwiches or cakes to eat; I felt out of my depth. Every time I stopped eating, Ian would encourage me to help myself to more; I took more not out of greed but to be polite, because he insisted that it was his treat to me.

As stories of Eva continued, I began to feel more and more inadequate. I was embarrassed about my less than perfect figure, plus my choice of outfit and hair. Every mouthful made me feel greedy and just when I was beginning to feel that the date couldn't get any worse, Ian suggested that I would benefit from giving up carbs to lose a few pounds; I still had cake in my mouth, and it was literally very difficult to swallow.

I was so shocked by his comment that I didn't know how to respond. For a split second I considered it was a very inappropriate joke. However, he showed no sign of it being a pun and the tone had been very matter of fact; it had rolled off his tongue as easily as speaking about the weather. This confused me because I couldn't calculate whether he was trying to be rude or whether I had misunderstood what he had said.

Ian dropped me back at work and I spent the afternoon feeling oddly assaulted as if I'd been through an unpleasant ordeal and yet, I couldn't really pinpoint why. But somehow, I managed to make excuses for the odd first date. I told myself that we were bound to talk about our late partners as we were both still healing from our individual losses. Likewise, while there had been the reference to my weight, he'd also presented the occasion as a treat; a gift to make me feel special. As a result, I decided that the fault lie with me: I wasn't worldly wise or experienced in relationships.

Nonetheless, I felt confident that it had been the first and only date that I would have with Ian; I felt that my obvious inadequacies would deter us from seeing each other again. As a result, I didn't even bother to mention the encounter with any of my close friends.

However, I was mistaken. A few days later, as soon as Ian had returned home from his business trip north, he made it very clear that he wanted to continue seeing me; according to him he felt that our first date had gone well. He suggested that we alternate our weekends; every other weekend, he would visit me in Leeds, and likewise, I would finish work on a Friday evening, collect Lauren from the childminder and drive to Devon. Both returning on a Sunday evening to our respective homes. His weekends in Leeds always coincided with Lauren staying with her birth father Mac.

I don't know how many times we saw each other before our relationship became intimate. Our first sexual encounter was in a hotel room close to where I lived. Ironically, the hotel was the intended wedding venue for Hugh and me. Ian booked the hotel room.

Lauren was staying with Mac and so I was able to return home from work and get ready for the date night. I was incredibly nervous especially as the invite to the hotel was somewhat unusual. Ian text me with the details of the hotel, including what time to meet and the room number. However, he also asked me to arrive with some specific items: a notebook and pen, a bottle of water, a packet of mints and a bin liner.

I couldn't help sharing my date news with my friend and colleague, Rachel; who on hearing the list of items, told me that she would never forgive me if I was stupid enough to turn up and ended up murdered and chopped into pieces; especially if I'd even provided my own bin bag for my disposal.

The conversation with Rachel seemed more absurd than the text. I didn't suspect a murderer would be so bold as to ask their victim to bring along a bin bag for such a purpose. Surely, my body would also require more than just one garbage sack. And yet, there was no logic for the request. It created discomfort and yet, alongside my unease, was a strange level of acceptance; a mental surrendering to *what will be will be.*

I believe that the trauma and circumstance surrounding Hugh's death meant that my boundaries had become severely warped. I had this deep feeling that after waking next to a dead body, nothing could ever be worse than that. To act fearless, felt like I was offering another two-fingered salute to God; a kind of 'bring it on' gesture, which motivated me to accept Ian's invite and to arrive at the hotel with the requested items. I didn't realise the level of my own vulnerability.

We started the evening with dinner, but due to nerves and wishing to avoid carbs, I had no appetite. Afterwards, we went to the hotel room which was beautiful, and I found myself wondering whether it was the honeymoon suite; the thought felt surreal and created a pang to feel loved again. Hugh had been the only person I'd ever truly felt loved by; he behaved in a way that said to the world that he was so proud and happy to have me in his life. He would often tell me that he felt like the luckiest man alive.

Sex with Ian was functionary. His mission was to ensure that I orgasmed several times but less for my satisfaction, but more so to enable him the kudos of stating how good he was in bed. It was all very practical and almost biological. It lacked love and affection; it felt like a means to an end, even though I had no idea what ending I was seeking.

Afterwards, Ian prided himself in the assumption that no one had ever made me orgasm so many times. While the statement was true, I felt a sense of shame and guilt that I had had sex in the hotel, potentially the room intended for my wedding night with Hugh. I was also deeply confused as to why an orgasm could even be achieved when there was no sense of love or affection in the act of intimacy. This made me feel oddly dirty. I could feel a desperate yearning to ask God for help, but I was adamant that I wouldn't speak to Him again; I was determined that I would be fearless and disregard my anxiety.

Subsequently, Ian told me that Eva had told him that he was the best lover she'd ever had; I had no response to that. Ian disappeared to take a shower; my initial thought was that he was hastily washing me off him. This further deepened my sense of shame. As I listened to the sound of the shower, I didn't feel good, but I was uncertain how I was supposed to feel. Any doubt, I put down to missing Hugh and the guilt that I felt after having sex with someone other than him. I kept telling myself that I must have enjoyed it because of the multiple orgasms, but I still felt a sense of being violated, which again, I blamed on my culpability.

I was also aware that I lacked confidence and disliked my body; this feeling was worsened when pregnancy gave me stretchmarks on my thighs and stomach. Mac had clearly been repulsed by my body post pregnancy, something he admitted during a 'honest' conversation and hence his affair with Dee. Seemingly, motherhood and my body were to blame for Mac seeking sex elsewhere. It hadn't been like that with Hugh; he made me feel safe.

Minutes later, I was invited to shower alone. I was instructed to use Ian's personal products; he told me to never trust the quality of goods offered in a second-rate hotel. Once more I found myself unsure as to whether I should feel complimented or offended. On the one hand he was allowing me to use his quality shower products, which felt personal, and yet, he was referring to the hotel that had been intended as my wedding venue as substandard. I was certain that I'd mentioned my marriage plans to him, but decided that if he'd known about them, he couldn't possibly be cruel enough to book the same hotel for a date night or to comment negatively about the location.

After my shower, I returned to the bedroom wrapped in a towel, I felt clumsy and awkward. Ian offered me a body lotion, which he said would be good for my dry skin; I was mortified that he'd even noticed. I was informed that the lotion had been Eva's favourite and could only be bought in Paris. He allowed me to keep the lotion. Another treat.

I don't know how I managed to sleep; I was still considering the conversation I'd had with Rachel: if the bin bag was to be put to use, I reckoned it would happen while I slept.

I woke the following morning to an empty bed. Ian was on the balcony drinking coffee and smoking a cigar. He had clearly been working on his laptop: I was surprised to see that his screensaver wasn't of Eva, but of another very beautiful woman.

He came into the room and offered to make me coffee, which I accepted. He spoke of driving me home as he needed to leave promptly after breakfast. I tried to be myself, to be more relaxed and light-hearted. I asked him why he had instructed me to bring along a selection of items, which hadn't been used. He asked if I had brought all of the items with me; I admitted that I had. He smiled to himself and said that the request had been his sense of humour.

While I dressed, I observed Ian as he went to retrieve his laptop. I casually enquired who the woman was on his screensaver; I didn't mention that I found it odd that it wasn't an image of Eva. I was informed that the woman was called Noelia, and that she was a French actress and Eva's best friend. He went on to tell me that Noelia had been an angel during Eva's illness; he spoke of how she had travelled to the UK from Paris to help with her care. After Eva's death they had remained good friends.

Moving on from the initial date night, Noelia along with Eva, became a regular topic of conversation during our weekends. Ian would regularly reflect on his adoration for them both; I would brush off my feelings of insufficiency believing that he was entitled to share his memories with me. It wasn't his fault that talk of their beauty, education, career, success, and ambition made me feel deeply flawed.

I was also informed that Noelia had invited Ian to visit her in Paris. According to him, she liked to walk around her apartment naked, which he stated, was very typical French behaviour; he said that French women were outwardly more sexually confident.

His comments about Noelia stirred feelings of inadequacy; it was a big deal for me to be sexually active with him, especially as I lacked body confidence. But he would always seem to sense my change of mood and offer me a timely compliment. He would tell me that regardless of what Noelia had to offer, he recognised that I was 'sweet' and 'gentle'. He suggested that we were destined to meet. He emphasised that once he had made up his mind about someone, that he would be committed to them forever. He told me that he believed that I was his soulmate. I had thought Hugh was my soulmate, but his death made me doubt whether this was true.

We continued to alternate weekends between Leeds and Devon. When I visited him in the southwest, we each had separate bedrooms. The idea behind the separate bedrooms was for Lauren to not find us in the same bed; it felt too early for that after Hugh. This felt respectful and the right thing to do at that time. We would have sex in my room, the master bedroom, and Ian would return to his bedroom afterwards. Sex was always the same mechanical pattern; he would pride himself in his abilities to give women what they wanted. I continued to think I was sexually lacking because it didn't feel how I wanted or expected it to feel.

Any doubts I had regarding the relationship with Ian, would be quickly rectified when Ian would take Lauren and I for drives across Dartmoor to wonderful hotels and seafood restaurants. It was all very luxurious and well-planned to make sure the day was as child-friendly as possible. The trips were often very magical and picture perfect, which made it easy to ignore the niggling feeling that I felt uneasy around Ian. I would brush off any negative thoughts as old thought patterns; blaming my past, flaws, and vulnerabilities for creating my sense of unease.

Every time Ian and I met, he would shower me with gifts that made me feel very special. He bought me cashmere scarves and jumpers from Paris. He would present me with expensive perfume and French chocolates. Offer me bouquets of yellow roses. Every time I visited his home, he would leave a romantic poem on my pillow. He would cook dinner and introduce me to champagne and delicacies I had never tasted. I learnt that many of these gifts had been Eva's favourite. But instead of feeling offended that he didn't seek to buy me gifts that better met with my preferences, I began to believe that I had the potential to be as beautiful and loved as Eva. The gifts made me feel worthy.

I wasn't seeking, nor did I need a 'sugar daddy' figure. I had a professional job in media, I had the house that Hugh and I had bought. I had also received a substantial pay-out from Hugh's life insurance policy. Therefore, I was more than financially capable of taking care of myself. But what death did to me was make me re-evaluate what was important in life. I wanted to be loved. I wanted a family and a sense of home. I wanted to belong. I wanted to feel safe. I wanted all of the same and more for Lauren, too.

I wear my heart on my sleeve. Therefore, I don't doubt that I was always very open and honest with Ian. I would have shared with him my deep thoughts on re-evaluating my life and the priorities I felt as a mother to give more time to Lauren.

As a result, Ian started to fuel fear regarding my long-term financial status and ability to juggle, single parenthood with a demanding career. He would speak of my earning potential and how the money from Hugh's life insurance, wouldn't last long; it was true, paying a mortgage, childcare and travel expenses almost negated the purpose of going to work.

Ian also condemned the house that Hugh and I had bought; he said that it was squalid, Hugh and I had found it quirky. His words upset me, but then he turned the insult around to make it appear that he was just looking out for me. He added that he was concerned about how I would be able to maintain the house long-term; it was an old cottage that required a lot of work.

On the subject of my career, Ian boasted that he would never be a slave to any employer; he was ambitious and being self-employed meant that he could drive his own success, choose his own working hours and salary. With his help, I could do that too: I could be ambitious and successful; we would do it together, because he loved me

Likewise, he reminded me that my friend and colleague, Rachel, was a single parent and she'd spent most of her media career fighting with management over her inability to cover 24/7 shifts. I was appreciative of finding a childminder via Lauren's playschool, but I was aware that there were no guarantee that this was an arrangement that would last for as long I needed.

Aside this, Mac was being very difficult. He didn't like the fact that I had a new man in my life. It seemed okay for him to have had an affair and to move in with the woman in question, Dee; but for me, it appeared that it wasn't right to have a 'strange man' hanging around my home and more specifically, our daughter.

On several occasions, when Mac knew that I was with Ian, he would call me and tell me that I needed to get home because 'my daughter' was sick and needed her mother. I would receive phone calls from my ex-mother-in-law telling me that I needed to quit my job and become a full-time mum; she would tell me that it was time for me to put motherhood before my 'precious' career. This was while at the same time, Mac claimed that he was unable to pay child support, but both he and his mum deemed it necessary that I stopped working.

The first Christmas after Hugh's passing, I had just returned to work and was scheduled to direct a live outside broadcast (OB) that would feature a school choir, an appearance from Santa Claus and various interviews with shop owners discussing seasonal trade. I was in the OB truck when the floor manager (FM) informed me that I needed to go on set immediately.

Mac who was supposed to be caring for Lauren until the end of my shift, had arrived on set, and basically dumped her, claiming that he had other commitments. I later learnt that he'd made plans to take Dee out for dinner. Thankfully, the FM was amazing and arranged for Lauren to sit with Santa Claus while I directed the show.

Nonetheless, I felt pressure from all sides. I began to feel anxious and there were moments when I was driving, and I would be overcome with panic. I started to worry that I couldn't survive on my own; I began to create 'what if's' in my mind: what if I lost my job? What if I lost my home? What if I became ill? What if I couldn't take care of Lauren? On top of all this, I was still grieving and suffering from the traumatic events surrounding Hugh's death. I was vulnerable, which made it easy to be swayed by the strong opinions of others into believing that I couldn't have it all. All of which, further fuelled Ian's claim that I needed to be rescued.

It took the advice of Walt and Maria, to help me see that Ian orchestrated a slow drip of negative comments that fuelled my anxiety, stirred the fight or flight mode within me; then just as I was sinking into a bad place, he would offer something, the proverbial golden carrot that placed him in the role of saviour, my knight in shining armour. I was blinded by fear and grief, to his regular pattern of destroying and rebuilding my emotions.

The timeline from meeting Ian to leaving my home, career, family, and friends; relocating from Leeds to Devon was 8 weeks. Just two months! It was that quick. I gave everything up because it felt like the entire world was conspiring against me. Sadly, my workplace didn't even attempt to convince me to stay. I was disposable, just another potential liability as a single-parent. Ian had avoided meeting my friends, which meant that they bought into my romantic version of our relationship; they believed I deserved to be swept off my feet. Thus, I gave it all up to start a new life and to chase love.

Therefore, I wasn't just swept off my feet; I was knocked off my feet by a forceful energy that pushed me into a choreographed long-term commitment. I wasn't aware that what felt like flattery and a form of intense devotion, was part of Ian's plan to rush into a commitment, so as to secure me into the relationship. Ian knew exactly what he was doing and what narrative to use on me; he led me to believe that I needed to be rescued and that he was the one to do that. His mission in life, the knight in shining armour, was to be my provider and protector; in my vulnerable state, I believed him.

Maria also stated, fast-tracking commitment is a calculated strategy to create a sense of obligation, which then makes it harder for the victim to leave. He toyed with my fight and flight senses, knowing that I would opt to leave everything that in reality had offered me stability; he mentally deconstructed my stability to make it all feel unsafe. As a result, I chose to flee carrying my young under my wing, but I flew directly into the lion's den.

> 'Love bombing isn't just excessive amounts of attention. It can also be verbal adoration that comes without any real evidence that they know you to be how special they say you are. It's making a person feel extraordinary before knowing if they are actually extraordinary. It's making a person feel like they can give 100% trust before trust has been established. Love bombing is sometimes just manipulating a person into having complete faith and trust without having to prove they actually deserve it.'
>
> **[Source: Ash Taylor]**

> 'Love is nothing without action.
> Trust is nothing without proof.
> And sorry is nothing without change.'
>
> *[Source: Unknown]*

2

Red Flags: Gaslighting / Isolation from Others

The behavioural cycle of a narcissist is a predictable, yet distressing loop that encompasses phases of ego threat, abusive behaviour, playing the victim, and empowerment. When their fragile ego is threatened, a narcissist reacts defensively, resorting to various forms of abuse to regain control. As tensions escalate, they deftly play the victim, twisting facts and evoking sympathy. This power play manipulates the victim into accepting blame, bolstering the narcissist's perceived superiority. Ultimately, feeling vindicated and empowered, they thrive on this cycle, repeating it whenever their dominance is at stake. This cycle perpetuates the toxic dynamic, entrapping the victim in an endless emotional rollercoaster.

Therefore, the overall objective of a narcissist is to control and manipulate their victim. There are many different forms of control and manipulation, one such term is gaslighting, which is defined as a tool for then to maintain power over their victims by undermining their confidence, self-esteem, and sense of reality.

In my case, gaslighting had already begun during the love-bombing process; my confidence had taken a battering and I'd lost all sense of reality. I'd gone from independent professional career woman to someone who believed that I wasn't able to survive on my own. I was scared and vulnerable. I couldn't see what was happening to me. I was completely blinded by a feeling that I needed to be rescued and that Ian was the knight in shining armour who would enable that to happen.

I became completely incapable of using my own common sense to evaluate the situation. It was pure madness to up and leave my job, home, and friends, to relocate after knowing Ian for only 8 weeks. My workplace had given me a send-off and quickly my shoes were filled by the next person wishing to pursue a media career. So deep was my trauma I didn't even stop to think about negotiating part-time hours, a pay-off or to secure shares and my pension. I couldn't think long-term, I didn't have a weeklong plan never mind a one-year or five-year strategy.

Likewise, it was sheer craziness to uproot my traumatised and grieving daughter, to a new home hundreds of miles away, limiting access to her birth father Mac and his family. But I allowed it to happen because I was a vulnerable target. Many friends and the people who offered support after Hugh's death, had moved on; the phone calls checking on Lauren and my wellbeing had long stopped.

There was also a large black cloud gathering within Mac's family regarding my decision to leave Yorkshire for Devon. My fear ran far too deep to even consider that they had a valid point. Mac's family had always had their own narrative about me. I was always deemed to bring trouble to their door due to my upbringing, a reference to my mother's depression, and alcohol abuse. There was no care from Mac's family, just judgement: no one saw the young woman I was, who so desperately needed help. It was so easy to run away from all of that; to start a new life. I felt like a lone wolf with no one to turn to other than Ian.

I was crumbling and as a result, Ian's offer to take sanctuary in Devon seemed like a good idea. The county is stunningly beautiful with its miles of coastline, rugged moorland, and mystical tors. Ian had a house on the coast, you could see the sea from the bedroom window. On a morning you could wake to the sound of seagulls or the distant sound of a ship's horn. There was colourful beach huts, crab and shellfish food shacks, promenades, fishing boats and candy floss. My few happy memories of childhood had evolved around the seaside: I expected to be happy again. I wanted the same and more for Lauren.

I travelled to Devon with what I could fit into the back of my car, which wanting to ensure Lauren didn't leave behind any of her favourite toys or books, did limit what I could take for myself. But I did take what mattered to me, including my collection of angels and

Hugh's guitar. Plus, I always had the option to do a return trip to collect more belongings; but, in the back of my mind, I didn't think I was able. My home in Leeds was shrouded in bad memories, I couldn't visit a single place that didn't remind me of Hugh and the tragic events surrounding his death: all of which contributed to the ease of leaving it all behind. Additionally, Ian's home had everything we could possibly need; I didn't own anything that he wanted or desired in his house, therefore, Lauren and I only took necessities. Everything else was to stay in the house in Yorkshire until I decided what to do with the property.

However, after I moved to Devon with Lauren, everything seemed to change rapidly. Sharing a house with Ian, was how I imagined it would feel like moving permanently into a B&B. We were shown our bedroom and bathroom, plus other facilities, and then left to make ourselves comfortable. As considerate house guests, I encouraged Lauren to tiptoe around the house so as not to disturb the other guest, Ian. Likewise, to leave our rooms tidy in case housekeeping visited.

Similarly, if the establishment's owner was ensconced in his office, we needed to be as quiet as mice so as not to intrude on his working day; we didn't listen to music or watch TV in case it was an inconvenience. I didn't feel like we'd moved in with Ian, it felt like we were house guests.

There was never what I could call a honeymoon period; overnight, all of Ian's romantic gestures stopped. I realise that this phase cannot continue indefinitely, but as soon as I stepped over the threshold into my new life living with Ian, it was as if he literally believed, that he didn't have to try to romanticise me anymore. All the gestures such as love poems, cooking dinner with me or for me, and the gifts of perfume, cashmere, and roses, simply stopped. Instead, gifts slowly became part of a reward system.

Lauren was given her own bedroom, which allowed her to have her own space, but her belongings were to never spill out into the rest of the house. Lauren was allowed to play with her toys around the home, as long as the routine was to put them away afterwards, which didn't seem unfair. As for me, Ian didn't allow me any space within his home to store or place anything that I valued. It was as if everything I owned, didn't match with his quality standards. Hence, my collection of angels, that brought me comfort, were viewed as tacky and were banished to a bottom drawer. He hated framed photographs, so I wasn't allowed to hang or place them around the house. This rule extended to a single print I had bought while travelling with Hugh. I also had a favourite mug he had bought me; I have no idea what happened to this.

I don't doubt that Ian would strongly deny my claims that he didn't permit me space to place personal belongings; it depends on our individual definition of what is space. He offered me a workspace in the corner of the dining room, which was accessed via a small archway, which gave it a feeling of being an almost separate room. I'd never had a home office before. I wasn't working, therefore, it inspired me to think of how I could use the space. I had always wanted to write, and once Lauren went to school, I realised that I could consider this further.

While I was able to find a glimmer of inspiration in the workspace offering, the office was decorated with Eva's personal belongings, which I was invited to use, but instructed not to remove. Notably, Eva had framed photographs of her with Ian and Noelia decorating the walls.

The second space allocated to me was Eva's dressing room, which was also crammed with her belongings. I didn't judge Ian for this as I'd found it very difficult to part with Hugh's personal belongings, including his clothes. However, we were both supposed to be starting over. So, it hurt that I had uprooted my entire life to be with Ian, and yet, he'd made no effort to even create, in a room with four wardrobes and two chest of drawers, space for me to place my clothes. Instead, I was invited to squeeze myself in and around Eva; Ian even incited that I was allowed to wear her clothes if I wanted to, but again, the request wasn't to permanently remove them. Conspicuously, more framed photos of Eva, Noelia and Ian peered down from the walls of the dressing room.

Along with the instruction to not remove the wardrobe items, I was reminded that Eva's outfits came from Paris, it was the clothes she wore for her high-powered PR role. She could afford luxury and Ian claimed that it would be such a shame to give it all away or for them to not be worn. It was true, Eva's clothes were stunning, but I felt mocked by the invite to wear them; Ian had hinted on numerous occasions that I needed to lose a few pounds and he knew all too well, that her clothes wouldn't fit me. Inferiority was beginning to strike, and this made me feel guilty for feeling this way because Eva was dead and yet, I was begrudging her perfection.

I didn't feel that I could discuss my feelings with Ian: I didn't want to appear jealous; I felt that to be envious was an ugly trait especially when focused on a deceased woman. I also knew that Ian was potentially still grieving, so it felt unfair to expect him to remove her belongings to make way for mine. Sadly, I didn't know how to negotiate a balance that would help me to feel more welcome; I was one of life's well-attuned people-pleasers.

As a result, because I blamed myself for feeling the way that I did, it meant that no internal alarm bell rang to warn me to get out of there. I simply took it all in. I truly believed that the problem lie with me. I was the one with the growing inferiority complex. I was the one who didn't feel good enough. I was the one who needed to work on myself; Ian was just grieving.

It was in Eva's office that I discovered Ian's first lie. You could say that it was unimportant, but I found an ID belonging to Eva in a pencil box, which revealed her age. Ian had said that she was the same age as me. Her age was of no importance to me personally; however, I didn't understand why he'd hidden the fact that she was actually ten years older than me. It seemed odd that he would lie; what did he gain other than to give the impression that he always dated women who were 20-years his junior.

Ian had previously mentioned that he had a space in his home office where he kept Eva's personal paperwork. Therefore, on finding the ID, I handed it to him so that he could file it with the rest of her papers. He seemed surprised that it had been left where I could find it; he appeared to double check my story and questioned if I had really found it on the desk in my office space. I assured him that I had. I could feel my face flushing as he had the tendency to make me feel guilty even when I was totally innocent.

Irrespectively, I wasn't a liar, and I didn't like him questioning my honesty. From somewhere, I found a rare moral defiance that allowed me to bravely point out to him that I had noticed Eva's date of birth on the identity card; I questioned her age, reminding him that he'd told me that she was the same age as me.

It was then that I saw something in his face that said that he didn't like being challenged. The look was enough to make me feel uneasy. His response was to tell me that I was mistaken. I told him that it wasn't something I would get confused, and this rattled him. He denied ever telling me that Eva was my age and stated that I was clearly getting muddled with the other women he had dated since Eva's death.

Other women?

I had thought I was only competing with Noelia. I couldn't contain my surprise and asked,

'What other women?'

Ian kept his response short while continuing to seemingly work on his computer. He said that he had dated a few and his favourite had been the Meg Ryan lookalike, who had shown great potential. I was certain that I'd told him a story about how I once asked my hairdresser to give me a Meg Ryan hairstyle, because she was one of my favourite actresses. I couldn't be sure, but I wore my heart on my sleeve with him, which meant that I was very open and honest; therefore, I could have told him anything. Nonetheless, confusion as to what had or hadn't been said was beginning to evolve.

Ian continued to work on his computer and the silent treatment began. I was left hanging and uncertain what to do; it was clear that the conversation was over. I cautiously went back to Eva's study space, which was allegedly mine, and sat in silence. Ian normally worked from behind a closed office door, but on this occasion, he left it open; it felt like he wanted me to know that he was watching me. I felt scared and confused. And yet, such a sense of guilt that I had potentially mistaken Eva's age and in doing so, had upset Ian.

Sometime later, only after the silence had stirred unbelievable levels of fear and anxiety, Ian called me into his office with the offer of joining him for a coffee; he wanted to stop work to have a cigar with the beverage. My instant reaction was to believe that he was offering me an olive branch after our small disagreement. His office was his private space, and I was only supposed to enter if invited, therefore, I was grateful for the offer and accepted the invite.

I took a seat in a leather armchair, which sat next to a large window with views toward the coastline. I drank coffee while listening with interest as Ian introduced me to some of the contents of his desk drawers. Again, I was told that he didn't often share this information with just anyone. Ian liked cigars, so he showed me a collection of lighters; notably he mentioned that an expensive Dupont was a gift from Eva. He also had an assortment of beautiful pens, a small humidor containing a selection of Cuban cigars, cufflinks and then a penknife. Everything had a story attached to it and I was just beginning to feel comfortable, as though this was Ian's attempt of a peace offering, when he began to talk about how his office was extremely private.

He stated that his privacy was important to him and that if anyone, which he emphasised again, 'anyone' ever snooped around his office there would consequences. He said that he couldn't be with anyone who betrayed that trust.

While on the one hand, I agree that it would be wrong to snoop into anyone's private belongings without consent and I understood fully the need for him to make his boundaries clear to me. But it was the timing of the invite that felt like he was shooting a warning in my direction, because he clearly still didn't believe that Eva's ID had been left in a place for me to find. The caution served only to make me feel as though I was easily disposable: no second chance if I should ever mess up, which isn't the makings of a strong and loving partnership.

He then introduced me to another of his prize possessions, which was a serrated hunting knife that he claimed was the one that he'd used in the military. He went on to tell me how to use the knife to kill someone; he stated that a knife was close and personal, and that his military training had taught him that once you go into combat with a knife, it is a case of kill or be killed.

Even though Ian wasn't directly threatening me, I felt really uneasy. Ian was good at being subtle; he had a gift for presenting things in a way that when reading between the lines felt disturbing but was so indirect, he could always claim immunity, a form of plausible deniability. Because of this form of behaviour, I soon began to find myself in a constant state of uncertainty of what was happening: Ian was either very clever or I was highly paranoid.

Another strange conversation we had during another invite to join Ian in his office, related to something he called 'third party referral'. He explained that it worked in a way whereby you have a conversation with a person and to get your point across to them, you use a third-party person. The example he gave me was to talk to a person about someone else's negative features in the hope that they would realise that you were referring to them.

From that day on, Ian would almost daily, make statements that could potentially be a third-party referral incident. We could be watching TV or in a café eating breakfast and he would make statements about another woman. He would say things like,

"Look at the state of her, she's too fat for that outfit."

Or,

"She looks like she's eaten all of the pies."

I felt like I was beginning to go crazy. On the one hand I was thinking to myself, that surely no-one, including Ian, could ever be mean enough to share 'the third-party' referral tactic story and then so blatantly use it against me; to insult me. But it was every single day. Every day that I was with him, he always had something to say, always, about another woman. Never a man. And it was always derogatory.

"Look at her hair… it's over bleached and looks fake."

"She doesn't know how to behave…"

"Listen to how she speaks, she's clearly an imbecile…"

"She's uneducated."

"Look at her stuffing her face, she eats like a pig."

I became so nervous, that I would always be worried about how I presented myself, how I ate, how I looked and how I spoke. And yet, I had no real evidence that the insults were intended for me.

I had moved to Devon for love and happiness and yet, quite quickly, it was beginning to turn into a living hell. I felt confused, my self-esteem and confidence were at an all-time low and I had lost my sense of reality. I was unaware that I was being gaslighted and instead looked within myself to find blame.

My anger with God was further cemented because I couldn't understand what I'd ever done so wrong to deserve what was happening to me; why the punishment would extend to Lauren. My understanding of God was clearly of an entity that should be feared and who dispersed penalties at a whim. It even crossed my mind that perhaps I was being punished for stating that I no longer wanted to speak to Him; the decline in my state of mind and well-being was willing to consider any explanation.

Regardless, I'd only been living in the southwest for less than two weeks, but already I felt that there was no point of return. I had no one to talk to. I had burnt a lot of bridges to move to Devon. I didn't want to uproot Lauren, she seemed happy. As a mum, I was able to take her to playschool and make dinner on an evening, on weekends we'd go to the beach. She was making friends and thankfully seemingly unaware of the behind the scenes complexities.

Additionally, I was able to console myself with the idea that perhaps Ian was simply grieving the loss of Eva, as I still mourned for Hugh. I told myself that it was early days and that we both just needed time to adapt.

For the first few months after arriving in Devon, I stayed in contact with several of my closest friends and ex colleagues. However, this too was soon to become an issue when Ian presented me with an itemised phone bill and wanted to know 'who' was making calls to a Manchester number and staying on the phone for over one hour. Lauren occasionally spoke to Mac in Leeds on the phone, which Ian knew, but as there was no one else in the house, it was obviously calls that I had made.

I'd been calling one of my closest friends and work colleague Niks who used to commute daily from Manchester to Leeds. We did the same job, were on the same team and her mum knitted outfits for Lauren when she was born. Niks went on to have three daughters of her own.

Nonetheless, I was made to feel guilty over the length and cost of the phone calls. The only way I could resolve the issue, was to offer to pay for my own phone bills. In response, Ian told me to keep my money as I may need it one day, leaving me further wondering whether the comment was a threat or me being paranoid.

Needless to say, I limited the number of outgoing phone calls. I was becoming isolated. I had no direct family of my own and unless friends called me, I rarely spoke to them. This resulted in a number of my Yorkshire friendships ending. Ian appeared to have no local friends and he didn't speak to the neighbours, but he would often speak of other friends and business acquaintances, but I wasn't introduced to them, as they were mainly based in London.

It also took me until the end of our relationship to also recognise that the isolation had also crept into how Ian chose to sleep separately from me. Seemingly, this was my fault too. I hadn't questioned having separate bedrooms when Lauren and I had been weekend visitors, but we were in a committed relationship and therefore, it felt odd that we would continue to sleep in separate rooms.

According to Ian, I was too fidgety and made it difficult for him to sleep. It was true, I was restless at night, I was still traumatised from waking up next to Hugh's dead body; night-time felt unsafe. What I needed was for someone to hold me until I fell asleep and to do this until the night felt safe again. Instead, I went to bed alone and woke alone. I felt alone.

Ian initially worked from home, but within the first month, he returned to a more regular pattern of going away on business trips. In a way this gave me a little bit of a respite from him, but at the same time, I was further isolated.

Lauren attended playschool and I didn't feel able to make friends with any of the other mums. Ian had made it clear that he found mums that talked incessantly about their children dull. He also didn't like the idea of too many children within his home, therefore, how could I make friends with other women of my age with children. Again, I would console myself with self-platitudes; tell myself that I was lucky to be with Ian because he had chosen to be with me, even though I was a single parent.

What I didn't realise, is that I was beginning to even think like him; to internalise what he was saying to me. That somehow, I was being programmed to believe I was lucky to have someone like Ian in my life. But I guess it's understandable for this to happen when I was a daily victim of the 'third party referral' mind game. I was constantly being programmed to view women with similar features to my own, as being too fat, too ugly, too old and that these attributes made me unlovable. I needed to be grateful that anyone was willing to take me on, especially as a single-parent. Ian was a master of control and manipulation to the extent that he was able to ensure that I expressed no boundaries toward him. This meant that with no restrictions or rules on how he should treat me, I normalised his behaviour, which blinded me to the red flags of silent abuse. Combine that with a warped sense of faith and I was becoming one messed up person.

Ian had a cleaner called Vicky who came to the house weekly. When I first moved to Devon, I didn't get to meet her for weeks, as Ian would ensure that we were always out so that she could get on with her job. However, when Ian started to go away on regular business trips, I was home when Vicky came to clean. She was the only human contact I had apart from Lauren. So naturally, because I wanted and needed a friend, I was keen for us to get on with each other.

Quite quickly, Vicky and I began to chat with ease; I liked her a lot. However, I remained cautious because she had worked for Ian and Eva for several years, and it was evident that she had a lot of respect and loyalty toward them. While cleaning around Eva's belongings, Vicky would openly chat about Ian's late partner and tell me what she was like; the stories she shared were often quite different to the ones Ian had told me.

Ian had told me that he'd given up work to care for Eva when she became ill with cancer. He had spoken about how he had taken her to the best doctors, but they had failed her; not detected the cancer soon enough. As a result, he'd exhausted his funds, but had cared for her as best he could. I think it's important to add, that I really believed that Ian loved Eva, and that a great deal of care did exist; I don't want to take that away from them.

However, Vicky innocently spoke of how she herself and Ian's parents had rallied around to care for Eva, while Ian was away on business. She portrayed a man who claimed that he couldn't afford the time off work to care for Eva, if he did, the company would collapse. It had fallen upon Vicky and Ian's parents to support Eva in his absence. Eva's brother and friend Noelia had also visited from France, to periodically assist. I also learnt that Eva had worked in PR for a major drug company and that her medical insurance had paid for her treatments; this had enabled her to have access to some of the best doctors.

At the mention of Noelia as one of Eva's carers, I told Vicky that I'd heard the name and understood her to be a good friend of both Eva and Ian. I light-heartedly stated that Noelia had given me a run for my money in terms of pursuing Ian as a love interest. I was informed that Noelia was happily married and while she had done some small films in her youth, she loved being a wife and mum. It would seem that I was never competing with her. Obviously, I had no desire to tell Ian about my conversation with Vicky; the reprisal wasn't worth considering.

Some months later, both Ian and I were both at home when Vicky arrived, and it soon became clear that the two of us liked to chat to one another. Ian took me aside to tell me to 'not overly engage with the staff.' I admitted to him that I missed having friends and that she seemed nice. Ian told me that my way of thinking was naïve and not in keeping with the way prosperous people create success. He reminded me that she wasn't my friend and that she was there to work; he didn't want her to get paid to chat.

In some respect, I knew that he had a valid point, but again, I was left feeling as though I didn't belong in his 'grand' world. It was yet another series of comments that made me feel as though he was somehow more knowledgeable and experienced, and that if I wanted to better myself, I needed to listen to him. However, in the hindsight of writing these memoirs, it is still unclear to me, whether to state that he may have had a valid point regarding chatting to Vicky, is my view or his viewpoint. He managed to get into my head so much, that even now, I'm still trying to define what I believe and who I am on most levels.

Ian would return from his business trips to London and each time, he would share a series of stories about the wonderful hotel he'd stayed, the fine dining he'd experienced and the contacts he'd met with. Every trip he made, he would meet up with a female friend, Francesca, who in the twenty years I was with him, I never got to meet. I know she existed because I would hear her female voice on the phone when she spoke to Ian.

Seemingly, Ian had met Francesca, during his military career, and she knew of his past and the activities he'd done within that role. He made her sound like the character of M in the Bond movies as though she had access to state secrets. I realise how completely absurd this movie reference sounds: but this was a man who was very clever, charming, and persuasive. He never spoke in a way that came across as bragging. Instead, Ian appeared to be very laid back, and when he spoke and shared information, it would feel as though he was showing that he trusted me and that he was opening up to me. It made me feel accepted. Acceptance created safety.

Unlike Eva, Noelia and the Meg Ryan lookalike, Ian never used Francesca as a tool to make me feel sexually or physically inferior, instead she was the intellect, the intrigue, the person who knew him more than most as she was party to the 'secret operations' he claimed to have done; the 'wet jobs!'. Therefore, the more he appeared to peel back his many layers, the more I was made to feel as though he was confiding in me as deeply as he did Francesca.

Ian was entitled to have female friends and associates from whatever job he had done in the past. But what didn't sit right with me, is that he clearly shared information about me with her. As a result, he would pass back to me her advice. So, Francesca would send me information via Ian on how to deal with my eczema, or how to lose weight, the best exercises to slim down my thighs or if I was to visit London, the best colourist for my hair.

In my head this was telling me that he complained to this woman, who I never met, for twenty years, about the condition of my skin and hair and my physical appearance. What he was doing was just a more advanced and in-your-face form of the third-person referral game; tell an unknown woman about my flaws while dressing it up as friendly concern.

It was all getting too much for me. I really believed that I wasn't good enough for Ian and that he was having second thoughts about inviting me to share my life with him. But instead of focusing on what was right for Lauren and me, deciding whether I felt loved and appreciated enough, I fixated on what I had become to believe about myself. The character devised via third party referral mind games; full of endless flaws, worthless and unlovable.

I saw myself as overweight. I hated my accent; it made me sound uneducated. My hair had been over-coloured. I wasn't worldly wise. My clothes weren't fine. I was uneducated and could only speak one language and I struggled to be womanly.

If I ever showed any sign of feeling hurt about my growing list of flaws, Ian never offered reassurance, he would simply say,

"But I love you."

He often used these words as if he was some kind of consolation prize; wasn't I so lucky to have him regardless of my numerous faults, which he claimed to see through because love conquered all. Needless to say, I felt broken, and it was still only early days.

One day, I was feeling so insecure that during a lunch date, I asked Ian if he loved me. I asked, because the only time he said it was when he was doing the, you are flawed but I love you routine; he never spontaneously looked at me with love and told me he felt love for me. So, I asked him. I wasn't looking for confrontation. I spoke gently. I needed reassurance, but the question completely enraged him. His first response was to say,

"Not this again."

I was stunned. I'd never asked him this question before. So, I tried to explain that it was in fact the first time I'd ever asked, but he insisted that I was always asking him. I did try to defend myself and told him that that wasn't true; we hadn't been together that long and therefore, I'd had no reason to ask him the question before. In response, he stated that it was evident in my 'overall behaviour' that I'd been feeling this way because I was always 'insecure' and 'needy'. He told me to not take him for a fool and to remember that he was military trained, and he had interrogated terrorists and therefore, knew exactly what was going on with me. I then felt guilty and scared, because did this mean that he could sense that I felt hurt when he did his third-party referral routine, or spoke of Eva, Noelia, or Francesca.

He continued along the lines of,

"Don't I do enough to show you that I love you? Don't I provide you with a wonderful home, in an amazing location? You don't have to work. You live in luxury compared to how you used to live. Believe me, if I didn't love you, you would soon know about it."

I froze. I couldn't speak. I was scared. I was even scared of what would or could happen if he could read my thoughts and know that I was afraid. I didn't respond. Perhaps he expected an apology, but I worried that if it was not sincere, he would know. My silence seemed to infuriate him further. He stopped eating and threw down his cutlery. He got up to leave, saying,

"I've had enough of this."

He marched off to the car and left me terrified that he would drive off without me. So, I quickly paid for the meal and chased after him. I was petrified. I didn't want to be abandoned. I needed to feel safe. So, I began to question whether I'd behaved in a way that was disrespectful and lacked gratitude and so I apologised.

I was eventually allowed into his car, and we drove home in silence. My heart was racing, I was worried that he would end it and that Lauren and I, would be thrown out, discarded. All I could think of was what would this do to Lauren if I failed another relationship, how would she recover a third time? I needed to stick at it and to work on myself because if I hadn't been so full of doubt and insecurities, none of this would have happened. Everything was clearly my fault.

"The biggest gaslight of all is when people say, 'I love you and I want you' while trying to change who you are into what they want you to be."

[Source: Teal Swan]

3

Red Flag: Stonewalling

Again, there are fine overlaps within narcissist abuse, gaslighting can quickly move into stonewalling: every characteristic is a form devised to control and manipulate the target.

The silent treatment is a common tactic used by narcissists to stonewall their victims. They may stop talking to you, refuse to answer calls or text, or ignore you completely. This is their way of punishing their victim to assert their dominance. Another form of stonewalling is that they deny responsibility for their actions and deflect blame onto others, often shifting the blame onto you. All of which can fuel the victim's fear and anxiety, including low self-esteem and self-doubt.

Likewise, other examples of stonewalling are deliberately dismissing your concerns or questions. Abandonment. Changing the topic of conversation. Actively ignoring you while texting during a conversation. Therefore, when someone doesn't engage with you it can make you feel as though your thoughts don't matter.

I believed Ian was naturally a quiet person, which he often admitted, claiming it was due to his military service. He had explained that as a soldier, he needed to be still and observant. He had learnt to control the inner noise, the monkey chatter, as it could put a squaddie at risk during combat. It was a skill that he claimed he also used within his business, which was to always control his thought patterns; to never respond with a knee-jerk reaction to any issue or event.

I was led to believe that Ian wanted the responsibility for creating an abundant life for us as a family; that he was always thinking about what was best for us. Because of his apparent dedication to our family unit, it was easy to ignore any troubling thoughts I had about him, because I truly believed that beneath the surface that he genuinely did care for both Lauren and me. Therefore, my response was to always care for him in the only way I knew how to and in ways that I felt that he wanted or needed.

I remember as a teenager hearing one of my mum's friends complaining about men. She claimed that men expected women to be a Goddess in the kitchen and a whore in the bedroom; my mum agreed with the claim. This statement stayed with me forever; it acted as the only indirect advice my mum ever gave to me. Notably there is nothing wrong with enjoying either of these roles when it is completely consensual and both parties' needs are fully explored and appreciated.

However, blind to the silent abuse, I willingly became the perfect housewife, wife, and mother. I looked after the home, cooked meals, ironed his shirts and awaited his night-time visits. But I was in survival mode. Ever since I'd dared to ask Ian whether he loved me, it created an unbelievable amount of tension that left me walking on eggshells and with a heightened level of fear of abandonment. In addition to this, he continued daily to compare me with the other women and to play the third-party referral mind game.

I had an abusive childhood. My mum suffered from mental ill health. She mixed her medication with alcohol, and this had an impact on her mood. She would swing from extreme violence to remorse. Her violent state would see her physically attack my sister and I; it wasn't unusual for her to grab our heads and bang them against the wall, or to chase us with a kitchen knife. Afterwards, she would sink into deep levels of remorse that would seeing her crying, screaming, and at times, talking of suicide. She would cut her wrists, never deep enough to cause death but enough to gain attention and for us to feel guilty that she wanted to die; this fuelled my deep rooted fear of abandonment and confrontation.

I learnt in childhood how to placate my mum's violent moods to survive; I acquired the people-pleaser skill to avoid confrontation. I learnt that to cry or to question or to retaliate could be potentially dangerous. So, I had to know how to use my senses to read situations. This is a survival mechanism. But what these skills also did, was to finely attune my empathetic qualities, which has stayed with me for life. Anyone with a similar childhood may experience the same. Needless to say, Ian knew about my childhood fears and anxieties.

So, I became the dutiful, compliant, never confrontational wife, who rarely spoke and limited how often I shared my feelings. It was a twisted kind of reverse stonewalling; I was the silent one, but only because it felt enforced. I feared that I wouldn't be able to conceal my true feelings due to his claimed ability to read others well. I learnt to recognise Ian's different silent moods; the ones that were genuinely work-related versus those linked to me having said or done something inadvertently wrong.

I would continue to be invited into his home office whenever he took a break for a coffee and cigar. At times, I would just sit there, and he would ignore me while he tended to emails and texts. I guess there is an element of him that couldn't switch off from his work, but if I did try to leave his office to do something else, he would claim that he wanted me to stay because he liked me being there. I would always remain whenever he asked me to, as this fuelled my need to be wanted. I would allow this belief to override the fact that invariably I'd be ignored and left to sit in his room in silence. Like a dog, I'd wait at my master's side.

At times, he would take phone calls from his mother, Beryl. I would hear her ask him how Lauren and I were, but he would never tell me that his mother was enquiring about our well-being. Likewise, if phone calls seemed to be intense, he wouldn't share with me the content of what was happening. While I respected his privacy, it did feel as though he deliberately created uncertainty, which ultimately stimulated anxiety.

It became a common trend to never recognise what triggered an increase in anxiety, which made me permanently apprehensive and in a heightened state of unease. Without the ability to understand what caused me to feel this way, created a world that felt unsafe, and this further played on my insecurities and the need to believe that Ian was my provider and protector.

The more I believed that I needed Ian to survive, the more I normalised his behaviour to the extent that he was able to weaponise my self-doubt against me. He used the pain of my childhood and my relationship with my mum, to state that my present experiences were all in my head, insinuating that I was mentally unstable. Yet, before Ian, I was doing okay.

Nonetheless, with Ian, I had no friends or social life. I was never held or kissed. I went to bed alone every single night. Ian blamed the separate sleeping arrangement on my restlessness; an issue that was triggered by Hugh's death. Yet it was just another form of stonewalling.

If I ever made any suggestions or requests to do something differently, if Ian wasn't in agreement, there was never any room for discussion: it was his way or no way. Any hint that I was unhappy with this scenario would be met with a barrage of guilt-tripping; *'Don't you appreciate the life I've given you?'; 'Don't you realise how lucky you are?' 'If you're not happy, you know where the door is.'*

These phrases would also be followed by the silent treatment.

Sometimes, the silent treatment would lead into his business trips to London, where I didn't doubt, he would be sharing stories about me with Francesca, which further fuelled my feelings of inferiority, because I'd been made fully aware that she'd met Eva and had liked her very much.

When Ian departed for London during an incident of stonewalling, there was a pattern of him limiting his telephone calls to me, claiming that he was busy. If I tried to call him, he would subject me to shorter and more abrupt responsive conversations. Sometimes, he would cut me dead, even when he claimed to be having just a drink with Francesca. I would spend days in his absence feeling sick with worry. I equally hated confrontation and the silent treatment, which left me feeling tense until he returned home again. The conflict was the need to know whether we were still okay, and the only way I could establish this was to gauge his behaviour when he was with me because I didn't dare ask him direct.

At times, he would accuse me of not responding to his messages, which in a way turned the blame of stonewalling onto me. I would show him my phone to prove that I hadn't received a message to respond to from him. This is when he began to enhance the stories relating to his military career; tales that he'd been drafted from the Royal Marines to do covert work.

He claimed that Francesca was linked to this world, but I didn't know in what way. He stated that anyone associated with him would be of interest to these 'covert organisations' and he went as far as telling me that his phone calls and texts were being monitored, which could explain why they went missing, and why I wasn't receiving them. He created a sense of mystery and danger; his character would shift from hero to villain within seconds. His behaviour produced intense uncertainty, which overloaded my anxiety.

It soon became very clear that Ian didn't have any money of his own. Ian had a finger in a few pies business wise. When we first met, Ian ran a business with his brother Paul, that was sales related; eco solutions for industrial kitchens. However, Paul was seemingly only good for admin, which left Ian with the responsibility of sourcing clients, which in his opinion, made him vital to the business' success.

After leaving the military Ian had seemingly also been involved in investment banking, which had introduced him to the world of trade. Thus, his additional drive and ambition, aside to whatever business Ian ran with Paul, was to discover the ultimate trading platform to earn big money; to create billionaire success for the two of them. Therefore, the concept was for him to be a form of 'introducer' between investors and the platform that he was seeking and for Paul to carry out the relevant paperwork.

Nonetheless, trading platforms was a world that was totally alien to me and one that Francesca fully understood, which was the reason behind their acquaintance. Likewise, the purpose of Ian's regular trips to London, was to wine and dine business contacts in the hope of progressing the relationship to one with financial benefits.

It was odd that Ian had chosen to run a business with his brother, because he often referred to him has having sociopath tendencies. Ian claimed that while he brought numerous potential clients into the business, that many of the opportunities were ruined because of the way in which Paul treated them. He portrayed Paul has having high standards, not suffering fools gladly and that he could often be exacting and rude to people. If anyone crossed him, he would take them down. Therefore, whenever a business lead didn't progress, which was often the case, it was never Ian's fault; he would always blame Paul or someone else in the business chain.

At times, I would find myself in the firing line, even though I'd absolutely nothing to do with the business. If Ian was in the bathroom and his phone rang, he would ask me to answer. If I didn't answer in the way that he felt was professional and the content of the conversation didn't go to plan, then it was my fault for not greeting the client correctly. It was difficult to hide my absolute dismay and then this would lead back into the cycle of put downs, reminders that everything he was doing was for my and Lauren's benefit. I would then be guilt tripped and again this would lead into the silent treatment.

Ian never admitted that he had financial problems, but it soon became evident that things weren't good. He didn't use our home address for his mail; instead, all of his post went to his mother's house. He paid for everything on credit or would seek a loan from his brother. I learnt that his ex-wife was still paying for Ian's breakdown recovery and utility bills. When his daughter Olivia visited, she unintentionally shared information that indicated that Ian's money problems had been long standing, when she spoke of unpaid school fees. All of which was building an untrustworthy image of Ian, leading to further insecurities and confusion over what was the actual truth and yet, I was compelled to be completely silence.

Whatever the truth, and the stress behind that reality, it increased Ian's negative comments toward me and placed me as one of the people responsible for his hardships. He would complain about the need to warm the house while he was away in London. He would get annoyed with Lauren for leaving lights on after she'd left rooms, which is a common child problem and basically blame us for the costly pitfalls of having to care for a ready-made family.

I was living from the money left to me via Hugh's life insurance policy; I contributed to the cost of food, travel, and outings; I paid for Lauren's clothing, school trips and after-school activities. I still also had my home in Yorkshire, which did incur the cost of a mortgage each month, but at the same time, was increasing in equity. To appease Ian's complaints about the cost of supporting us, I asked him how I could help. I suggested I could rent out my home in Yorkshire to earn an income, which would cover the cost of the mortgage. I could then use the money I was no longer using to pay the mortgage toward our joint living expenditure.

However, my ideas were quickly shot down in flames. Ian claimed that my home would be impossible to rent out as it needed too much work doing to it; he thought it was squalid and wouldn't meet with the rental market requirements. Also, if I decided to do a private rental, I would potentially need to manage the property, which would require regular trips back to Yorkshire, which I couldn't do due to my parental responsibilities.

I then suggested that perhaps I could sell the house and buy something closer to Devon and rent that out instead. He told me that I would never raise enough money to purchase a property in Devon. So, I offered to go back to work and this time, I was told that whatever I was capable of earning wouldn't even scratch the surface of providing for our needs.

    I wanted to work, I wanted to have a purpose and to be with other people. So, I again, tiptoed around the issue and light-heartedly suggested that every little would help. He reiterated that Lauren was my responsibility and that he wouldn't help me with her childcare. This then pushed us back into the usual cycle of guilt tripping me over not appreciating what he was providing for me. Then he would add blame, because it was up to him to fix it, therefore, all of the pressure was on him, and he wasn't fully appreciated. More silence. More tension.

    Deep down I think I knew that I'd made a huge mistake leaving everything to be with Ian. However, time was passing so quickly, and I was getting sucked deeper and deeper into believing that I couldn't survive without him. I was still mourning for Hugh, which would intensify with every single one of Ian's jibes. Yet I longed to be loved and to have a sense of place and family. I wasn't really ready to sell my home in Yorkshire, but I was desperate to do anything to feel safe and wanted, which allowed me to continuously turn a blind eye to anything that could potentially stand in the way. Any disharmony I felt, I told myself I just needed time to heal or that it was my fault, and that I needed to adapt and change. If the thought of returning to Yorkshire ever felt appealing, I would return to the idea that I couldn't survive on my own: I was caught in a vicious circle. When Lauren started to call Ian, daddy, I couldn't be the one to destroy our family unit: I had to make it work.

    Therefore, while I was still confused and mulling over my options, Ian made a timely suggestion, which made it feel as though he could detect my growing doubt regarding our relationship. He offered to 'transfer' the ownership of the Devon house into my name so that Lauren and I, would always have a home. He stated that because he was twenty years my senior that if anything should happen to him, such as death, then at least I would have a house, with equity, that would take care of us and myself, in later life. He added that he wanted to show that he was 100% committed to us and our future.

Even though Ian's gesture seemed thoughtful, I was cautious and didn't respond immediately. So, Ian repeated the offer and re-emphasised the fact that he could die, and I could be alone and struggling. I didn't know whether he was trying to aggravate my fear of loss or being practical. So again, I was left in a confused state, whereby I didn't know whether I was being oversensitive and paranoid or being offered a very genuine and caring opportunity.

I found myself equally fearful of returning to Yorkshire and staying in Devon. The first was the place where Hugh had died and was full of sad memories; I risked living a life alone and having no work or support. Devon offered the chance of a family and home. So eventually, I thanked Ian for his wonderful offer.

However, the idea to take over ownership of the Devon house, came with various stipulations and new revelations. It turned out that the house Ian had always claimed was 'his home', he didn't own it. His ex-wife Jane was the registered owner, and the property was mortgaged to her. Thus, it was news to me that Jane was still paying the mortgage, while Ian and I lived at the house. I was told that she was on board with the idea of me taking over ownership. Jane was willing to sell the house for a none profit deal; all that she required was a purchase price that would clear all outstanding debt on the property.

To become the registered owner of the house, Ian advised that I needed to sell my home in Yorkshire as I wouldn't be able to meet with the cost of two mortgages. I didn't like the sound of Ian's plan, because not only did it force me into making a decision about my home in Leeds, but the new mortgage rate would also be triple what I was paying in Yorkshire. My family taught me very little that I can remember, but one part that stuck was the idea that if you cannot afford something, then it isn't meant for you: Ian would claim that this attitude is being small-minded. But as far I could see, I wasn't employed and therefore, didn't view it as a feasible plan to buy the house with no income, other than to use the life insurance money gained from Hugh's death, which would disappear rapidly paying a threefold debt.

I cautiously voiced my concerns regarding ownership of the Devon property to Ian, ensuring that I expressed my gratitude for the gesture. However, he was very good at getting what he wanted and persuaded me that to be on the property ladder in Devon, with a house that was already worth triple the amount of my little place in Yorkshire, would set me up for life if anything should happen to him.

He agreed that while it would swallow up some of the insurance money, he assured me that every payment I made was an investment. He stated that he would also pay toward the mortgage and that it wouldn't be left to me to meet with the cost alone. It did occur to me that his ex-wife was still paying the mortgage and I was curious to know why the property was not in their joint names; however, these were questions I dare not ask because I didn't want to anger him.

Detecting my uncertainty, Ian spoke to me in a way that I was getting all too familiar with; the words sounded caring and yet his eyes told me that he was losing his patience. Anger was brewing. He disliked having the validity of his gestures questioned. I listened as he reminded me that he was giving me what I wanted, because I had previously suggested selling the house in Yorkshire to purchase in Devon. He stated that as far as he was concerned, that I was not only getting a bargain for my money but also committed long-term security. He then went deafeningly silent. So, I did what I did best, I placated what felt like an unsafe situation by agreeing to sell my house. Once more, I felt silenced by the fear of his silence. Stonewalling is an extremely powerful control tactic.

I couldn't face saying farewell to the home I had shared with Hugh; it was too painful. As a result, I opted to sell my house fully furnished and allowed strangers to pack up the smaller items, which were given away to charity shops. Internally, I was emotionally distraught at letting memories shared with Hugh go, but I also didn't want to give Ian the satisfaction of seeing the pain it would cause me; staying away from the process felt like the best option. I also already felt that I had given away a lot of myself and I wanted my grief to be mine alone.

Ian arranged a mortgage for me via an acquaintance, who I later learnt had been in prison for fraud. However, the mortgage was with a major high street bank, so it appeared to be stable until I learnt that it was going to be an interest only agreement. My previous arrangement had an endowment policy, and while these can be unstable, it did mean that if there was any shortfall that the likelihood of finding a solution was more likely, than allowing myself to simply get into debt for something that was, more probably, always out of my financial reach.

The mortgage plan made me feel uneasy and I quickly felt out of my depth. I knew that to cross Ian would be unwise and detrimental to me, but I was scared and expressed my worries regarding being tied into the financial commitment of the Devon house. As I suspected, he viewed my uncertainty as ingratitude and mistrust; he was also extremely irritated by my small mindedness and for basically portraying that I didn't believe he was capable of earning enough money to clear the base debt.

He then twisted the conversation around to comparing himself to Mac and Hugh, claiming that it wasn't his fault that I was used to being with men who were failures. The comment literally stung, I felt like I had been physically slapped on my face. Neither Mac nor Hugh were failures; the latter was dead! Both worked hard in reputable and worthy careers.

I rightfully defended both as I couldn't allow Ian to speak with such disrespect for either as they had been part of my life, and both were father figures to Lauren. It took a lot for me to speak my truth, because I knew that the silence would be thunderous and that the threats of abandonment could become a reality.

Both Walt and Maria helped me to realise that it isn't normal to fear sharing concerns or a viewpoint within any relationship. Likewise, that the gesture of transferring ownership of the Devon property was never for my benefit but was a very typical narcissistic trait that allowed him to tie me into the relationship. Therefore, if I was to ever question his plan, he was always going to do whatever it took to maintain the situation, which was to revert to playing upon my fear of abandonment, which the stonewalling did, because sinister silence created uncertainty.

They also advised that it was likely that Ian's ex-wife had found the confidence to move on and had pushed to be free from paying for a house she no longer resided. It was possible that her experience of Ian was in part, similar to my own, but in her case, it had been difficult for Ian to take full control because her parents had lived locally; he hadn't progressed to the value of isolation until he had met both Eva and me.

To celebrate my ownership of the Devon property, I prepared a special family dinner; I wanted to assure Ian of my gratitude and to ensure that everything was fine between us. In doing so, it was necessary to explain to Lauren the purpose of our extra special family get together; so, I told her that I had bought the house and that it was going to be our forever home.

In all naivety Lauren asked,

"Does that mean he [referring to Ian] can't throw us out anymore? But you could throw him out if you wanted to?"

Such an innocent and damaging question at the same time. I think my heart skipped a beat because I really didn't know what or who to deal with first since suddenly all eyes were on me; Lauren's innocent gaze versus Ian's suppressed anger that was quickly rising to boiling point. I felt sad that I'd failed to protect my daughter from the fragility of the relationship of her parent figures. It was evident that she'd picked up on conversations, moods, and negativity. We'd failed to make her feel safe. At the same time, I also knew that I was in deep trouble with Ian.

Not so incredibly, Ian's reaction to Lauren's question wasn't one of concern but one of extreme anger. He truly believed that I'd put her up to asking the question; that I'd been talking to her about him in a harmful way. He couldn't see that I had no agenda for wanting her to be scared of her father figure especially after what she'd already been through. I wanted her to feel safe and to have a home and parents who were always there for her.

Regardless, the dinner came to an abrupt end. Lauren was sent to bed unsure of what she'd done wrong until I was able to calm her the following day. I wanted to go after her, but at the same time was torn between who to appease first. Under stress, I opted to prioritise what felt like the bigger danger, which was to deal with Ian's fury. Lauren was and still is a gentle soul, so I reckoned in that moment I could make it up to her, not realising that I was potentially fuelling her own sentiments of desertion and allowing her to fall asleep feeling anxious.

With Lauren in bed, Ian told me that if I thought that I would ever take his house from him to think again. I tried to reassure him that I would never speak disrespectfully about him to anyone, more so, Lauren. I tried to reason with him, that her comment suggested that she felt unsafe and that the only logic for this was because she had heard him telling me on occasions that I knew where the door was if I felt unhappy. But Ian denied ever saying this; instead, he told me that it was all in my head and that I had something wrong with me.

The following day, I offered some reassurance to Lauren that everything was fine and that we were safe. But she had already seen behind the masks, so I was uncertain whether my reassurances had any value to her anymore. As a parent I believe love and trust has to be earned; it cannot be an expectation and yet, I was making promises that I didn't even know whether I could uphold them. I was trying to appease fear and insecurity while being riddled with it myself.

The silence went on for days. I was constantly on tenterhooks not knowing whether Ian's simmering mood would explode. My mood was low, and my sense of worthlessness escalated; I was so unhappy. I stayed away from Ian as much as I could, but continued to be the perfect wife, caring for the house, ironing shirts and cooking dinner; I still felt the need to care for his needs because failure to do so could make the situation more precarious. Other than my duties, we acted like strangers

In my alone time, I started to write. I cannot remember what I wrote about at that time, but what I do know is that I would have never risked writing about my true feelings in case Ian ever read my words. Therefore, I would have opted to write fiction, which offered me escapism; I could create the life I wanted through storytelling. I used writing for the same purpose in my own childhood. I wrote stories about the adventures of a snail called Brian and a place called Alphabet Village. The characters I created became my friends, and I lived the life I desired, through them: they had the adventures and the bravery, the love and affection that was missing in my life. I repeated this writing pattern in my teen years too.

Since relocating to Devon, Lauren was unable to have regular access with Mac. As a result, she got to spend longer but less frequent periods of time with him. This meant that she often spent some of the school holidays with her father. Ian and I would arrange to meet him at a halfway point, and it worked well, because Lauren got to spend quality time with him.

We were due to meet Mac during the fallout regarding Lauren's innocent question; I didn't want to trouble Ian with the arrangement, so I planned to drive to the meeting point myself, but Ian insisted that he would drive. It was a difficult and silent trip.

Ian stayed in the car while I met with Mac and talked to him about Lauren; I was highly conscious of not appearing to be too pleasant with Mac in case it caused another argument with Ian. I noticed Mac kept glancing off toward Ian as if he could tell that things were strained.

We drove back home in silence, the only time I spoke was when I tried again, to reassure Ian that I would never speak in a derogatory way about him. His focus was to still deny that he had ever told me to leave the house, but he had, on several occasions.

Almost as soon as Ian had dropped me back home in Devon, he disappeared to London for the duration that Lauren was away. During this time, the phone calls were limited, and the content was cold and dismissive. I kept apologising. I was alone. I still had no friends. So, I buried myself in my writing and I joined the gym.

A week later, Ian volunteered to meet up with Mac at the usual rendezvous on his return trip from London; it made sense for him to collect Lauren enroute. He said nothing about the recent events and while it would have been healthier to discuss what had occurred so that we could both move on, I embraced this other form of silence, as it seemed safer.

It was soon to be my birthday, and so to my surprise, Lauren returned from her trip to Yorkshire with a gift for me. While staying with Mac, she had been to see her aunt, who worked in a bookshop. Her aunt had suggested that I may like the book, *There Is A Spiritual Solution to Every Problem* by Dr Wayne Dyer.

When married to Mac, his sister and I had always got on really well with each other; in fact, I knew his sister before I knew Lauren's father. We'd met while learning ballroom dancing; we shared the same teacher. However, my interest in spirituality occurred later, which made the gift perhaps one of the many synchronicities that goes unnoticed in everyday life. Nonetheless, I read the back of the book and it blew me away.

I finished reading the book in a day, and it was just the catalyst I needed to be inspired to reconnect with Source. The book quashed the feelings of loneliness I had, and it helped me to recognise that I was part of something much bigger than the life I was living. The book ultimately saved my life, as many great authors continued to do so, over the years, as the journey to reconnect and to stay true to my spiritual path recommenced.

I found the confidence to remove some of the angels from their hiding place and began to decorate my personal spaces with them. Immediately, I felt comforted and an overwhelming sense of being loved. I apologised to God, as I called him then, for being angry with Him; I knew in that moment that He had never given up on me and that it was time to have Him back in my life. I needed God to help me navigate life.

Psychology says:

> *'When you are ignored by a person whose attention means the most to you,*
> *the reaction in the brain will be similar to physical pain.'*

[Source: Various]

4

Red Flags: Excessive Need for Admiration / Grandiose Self Image / Entitlement

Narcissists have an unquenchable need for praise and recognition. In romantic relationships they may constantly demand compliments and reassurance from their partner. It fuels their inflated sense of superiority. It is highly likely that they will also have an inflated grandiose self-perception as well as outwardly flamboyant, characteristics. This creates an ego-centric person who will act with a sense of entitlement that requires for them to be treated as the central and most significant figure. This often makes their expectations and demands unreasonable. Often the narcissist will expect their needs and plans to always be prioritised above and beyond anyone else, even at the expense of their partner's own interests. If their needs aren't met with, this may result in a reaction of disdain or even anger.

Another pronounced narcissistic red flag is their strong sense of entitlement. Narcissists often feel they deserve special treatment and privileges, irrespective of the impact on others. This leads to a profound disrespect for other people's boundaries, and they often disregard the needs and feelings of others.

Therefore, in a romantic relationship, a narcissist might demand an excessive amount of your time, ignoring your personal needs or responsibilities. They may show little respect for your privacy or make decisions affecting both of you without your input.

In a family context, a narcissistic family member might take over family gatherings, imposing their preferences on everyone without considering others' wishes. They might disregard your requests for space or intrude on your personal life without invitation.

When it comes to friendships, a narcissist might expect you to always be available for them, disregarding your own schedule or commitments. They may consistently ask for favours without reciprocating or showing appreciation. Such blatant disregard for boundaries and persistent sense of entitlement are classic red flags of narcissism.

I never felt pressured to feed Ian's ego by telling him how amazing he was, because he fuelled his own self-esteem daily. He was the one who would tell me that he knew that he was handsome, good in bed, successful, wealthy, educated and extremely well-dressed. I viewed Ian as being confident and often wished I could be as self-assured.

Ian was full of stories that supported his self-absorption. He told me on many occasions of how Eva had told him that he was the best lover she'd ever had. In other tales, he would always have women chasing after him; including an American woman visiting London who allegedly offered him $1million to have sex with her. This incident seemingly happened while he was still married to his ex-wife Jane. He was keen to reiterate that once he had decided to be in a committed relationship that he would remain loyal; he stated that he had declined the offer.

Of course, Ian had also attended one of the best private schools, had excelled in the military, and had even been earmarked for elite covert work. After his Service career, he had been headhunted to work for a private bank and then went on to be a top salesman for another high ranked organisation. All of his suits, shirts and shoes were handmade on Jermyn Street, London. He had also stayed at the best hotels and had eaten in the top Michelin star restaurants. His home was decorated in the best and most expensive furnishings. The list was endless.

Ian's ideas were always grandiose, and he was driven by the desire to have a millionaire lifestyle; anything less was deemed as mediocre. I don't condemn anyone for having passion, drive, and ambition nor for gaining success. But with Ian he didn't have a clear plan on how to reach his destination; he was old school and operated in a system pre social media. He relied heavily on introductions, conversations, and wining and dining the right people.

I understand that many a deal is brokered over a meal and a glass of wine: that it is often who you know and not what you know. But in the two decades I was with him, my view of his world, was a man who tried to use others to propel himself to the dizzy heights he so desired.

Perhaps there is a naivety on my part; maybe a lot of the world evolves in this way. But it felt like he never brought anything solid to the table, he had no money or product, just pride and a sense that he was worth all the things that he wanted. To achieve his dreams, he depended on his appearance, his expensive watches, handmade clothes, and shoes. Eventually, this extended to the need to express his success and 'fake wealth' via the car he drove or the house he lived.

Every penny he earned funded his form of 'showmanship'; it subsidised his wardrobe, rental properties, and vehicles, but his mode of work didn't supply a regular income. He and his brother were self-employed, which naturally had its own peaks and troughs, but with the company being dependent on Ian as Head of Sales, it was hinged purely on him meeting the right people at the right time.

Both Ian and his brother Paul, were motivated by a quote from their grandfather, which was,

"Don't let anyone know that you're poor."

Seemingly, this was a man who they stated spent all of his money on fast cars, horses, and women. Notably, the list was always told in this order, the women coming after their grandfathers love for nice cars and racehorses. The joke would be that he lost all of his money because he often confused the three and ended up with too many 'fast women.' The humour was lost on me; I felt saddened that the derogatory reference to women was potentially within the family genes. Nonetheless, their role model for achieving success was somewhat dubious.

Beneath the surface there was no solid foundations to our life; everything was a front to attract private investors with links to elite investment platforms. A world Ian claimed he'd become familiar with during his covert military career. Nonetheless, while Ian chased his dreams, I was responsible for maintaining and securing the property in Devon; my funds were disappearing rapidly, and I would just keep telling myself that I was investing in our long-term future by holding the fort, while Ian focused on building the success of his business.

I believed that I was in love with this man, and I trusted that beneath the surface he felt the same way about me too. I didn't see the pattern of abuse; that fear of abandonment was slowly making me conform to living my life fully by his rules, which muted me from ever expressing my concerns. Instead, I normalised his behaviour, convinced myself that I needed to trust him as my provider and protector because this is what he wanted and needed from me. My people-pleaser characteristics prioritised his needs over my own, and potentially, that of Lauren who I continued to convince myself was too young to know what was going on in our lives.

When I conformed to Ian's way, I would occasionally get to meet some of his business acquaintances or to accompany him on one of his jaunts; this was my reward for compliancy.

Sometimes, I would be invited to attend after meeting drinks, where I got to meet some of his business contacts. On meeting his associates, it seemed notable that Ian did very little compared to them. I wouldn't question this direct, but if I commented that the person in question, a city trader, was never off their phone, hardly slept and seemed highly stressed, Ian would claim that they weren't in the same 'private club' as him.

Going on an outing with Ian, involved viewing the most magnificent properties, which was at a time when estate agents believed the word of a well-dressed city gent to be a genuine potential buyer; I guess in Ian's mind he was, because he believed that one day, he would be rich.

Thus, I've known property owners to fly in by helicopter to meet with us; myself included, the dutiful wife who played her part. I would be instructed to nod and smile when prompted and told not to speak as my accent may give away my lack of education. I was to let Ian do the talking because he claimed that I was prone to being too honest; I'd once admitted that our Hampshire pad was a rental property, and this had been a mistake.

Ian would be dressed for the role, every inch of him seemingly fitting with ease into the world of luxury homes. I would allow myself to be part of the charade and yet, I never felt like I fitted the role; I didn't own haute courtier clothing other than Eva's outfits that Ian had passed to me. Garments that I was still unable to wear due to my larger dress size, which meant that I would often find myself attending these farces wearing a pair of her expensive shoes or a scarf, with something I had bought from a charity shop. I felt like I was personally as equally farcical as the situation I found myself; an imposter wearing an outfit stolen from the props department of the local theatre company. During these outings, I would be subjected to Ian's disapproving look indicating that I had clearly failed to meet with his expectation. I would follow behind Ian allowing him to talk with the property sales Agent; somehow, if I walked behind them it lessened my visibility.

I would listen as Ian spoke to the Agent about his successful businesses, our *fake* Hampshire home and five-star lifestyle. He mostly talked about Eva and the life he'd had with her, but his words were never that of a man mourning the loss of a loved one. What he was doing was explaining the reason why he had ended up with someone like me; this overweight woman who looked out of place in this world of wealth. Ian wanted the Agent to know that he had once had better, someone more suitable. He sought the sympathy for his loss and used this as an excuse, an explanation, for my existence. He used his sob story to make himself more believable and likeable, which is probably why, he continued to invite me to these charades because he needed evidence of the existence of a wife to support his narrative.

And yet, this cruel set-up, would also offer another twist, in that it would be the only time he said anything that remotely resembled a compliment toward me. He would tell the tale of how in his grief, he had met me; a kind and big hearted gentle soul, who brought light into his life. He would then smile at me so warmly as would the Agent, a look of patronising 'how sweet.' I would be left holding on to the scrap of brief adoration, choosing to ignore that my unfitting presence needed to be explained.

I would later hear Ian talking to his brother Paul on the phone, about the properties we'd viewed. This would create a routine of one-upmanship between them; Paul would then send an email including details of the properties he planned to view. At this time, Paul was almost as unfamiliar to me as Ian's London female friend Francesca. They were both regular household names, but people I hadn't met.

As a result, Ian placed himself in control of my perception of others, which invariably he always created characters who I felt were untrustworthy or linked to precarious situations. Because I needed to feel safe, I would opt to believe that it was somehow better to know the devil himself rather than to trust a bunch of unsafe people, not realising that I was being manipulated into believing that I needed Ian for my safety and protection.

If I ever showed any signs of doubt, or an interest in meeting these people, he would simply diffuse any uncertainty by referring to Francesca in a derogatory way; his references to her weren't consistent. Likewise, he continued to alluding that his brother was a sociopath, while admitting that he needed Paul to help him run the business. I didn't see that this was Ian's way of protecting himself from any accountability if the business should ever fail.

My first direct introduction to Paul was when I answered Ian's phone while he was in the bathroom. His brother's first words to me were,

"You must be the wealthy widow… Ian has told me all about you."

I cannot understand why in that moment that no part of me recognised that I needed to get out of that relationship. There was no inner voice telling me to leave. However, I did know that somewhere in the depths of me, Paul's comment rung an alarm bell, which prompted me to find the courage to put Ian on the spot; to question why his brother had made such a statement.

But I should have known better, because I was never going to come out of a challenging situation with Ian unscathed. He reminded me that Paul was a sociopath who had a sadistic side to him. With this claim, Ian added that his brother gained great pleasure in creating unease. He confessed that while he perhaps shouldn't have shared my personal details with

Paul, that he had wanted to assure him that I wasn't a gold-digger, but in fact, had my own resources.

This was such a clever move on Ian's part. It further fuelled my negative perception of Paul, increased my levels of fear, which drove me deeper into the need and belief that a world away from Ian was unsafe. Likewise, Ian on the one hand had offered a back-handed apology by admitting he shouldn't have told his brother about my financial status; yet on the other hand, he was suggesting that he was also protecting me from the allegation of being a gold-digger.

Thus, not only did Ian manage to diffuse my initial unease, but he also succeeded in managing to turn the entire focus of the incident onto me. Clearly, he'd said something about my financial status to his brother and yet, he accomplished in remaining as the hero defending the gold-digging culprit, which caused me to worry that Ian may believe his brother over me; after all, he was family. Therefore, Ian could hold this allegation over me, so that I wouldn't expect anything from him for fear of strengthening the accusation. It further warped boundaries and normalised a deeply unhealthy and unnatural relationship.

Ian and his brother's quest to outdo the other's access to the millionaire lifestyle continued. Paul arranged for a private jet to be flown into Exeter airport on the pretence that the company needed one to make business trips more efficient. The plan had been to impress key business acquaintances during a short promotional flight along the north coast of Devon. However, no one accepted the invite and as a result, it turned into the oddest outing one can imagine. Not wishing to arrive without an entourage, Ian's mother, Beryl, Paul's wife, Iris, and myself, were recruited to make up the numbers. We were three women who hardly knew each other, but our purpose was to bolster the boys; to make all of the right supportive noises without revealing our true identities.

I found an odd comfort in discovering that Iris was even less equipped than myself for the absurdity of what was expected of us. Iris wore practical clothes that fitted her large solid frame; like Paul, she had required a seatbelt extension to be secured into her seat during take-off and landing. It isn't my wish to sound judgemental, but both their identities had been somewhat shrouded in mystery. Because of Ian, I'd been led to believe that Paul was someone to be feared. But regardless of his character, I had wrongly assumed that he would have a trophy wife, someone more like Eva, than myself. This showed the depths of Ian's control over my thoughts and emotions.

Iris didn't appear to be remotely fearful of her sociopathic husband, in fact, she referred to him affectionately as 'Pumpkin'. She happily tucked into the selection of on-board fine drinks and chocolates, while lovingly sharing her delight with her seemingly sadistic other half. Therefore, finally meeting them, allowed me to see that on the surface they appeared to be everyday people.

It was evident that Iris had clearly not understood the brief to not give away our identities as wives pretending to be important business contacts. However, I did catch a shared look of irritation regarding Iris' behaviour between Ian and Paul. For days afterwards, Ian complained about Iris, which I admit, I was secretly glad that the spotlight for once was on someone else other than myself. Iris was never invited on another fake business mission after that day.

The next grandiose venture was regarding Ian's love of prestigious cars, specifically Bentleys and Rolls Royce's. We would visit showrooms on a weekend, and I would listen to Ian telling a Sales Agent the usual tale of how he had met me after the death of his previous wife Eva. The Agent would offer the same sympathetic platitudes as Ian continued to promote himself as a hugely successful businessman who was indecisive about whether to buy a Bentley or a Rolls. As usual, I was encouraged to keep quiet, and to smile and nod when appropriate. Ian was extremely convincing, so much so, I've no idea how many hours the Agents spent with him, over the years, in the hope that one day he would choose to buy from them.

To encourage his decision, we were invited to some extremely prestigious no expense spared, free events, including a day at the races, a full day test driving Bentleys followed by cocktails, that included an evening talk by a famous author and then dinner at a 5 star restaurant. It was all very lavish and a world that is enjoyed by very few, but I felt like an imposter, listening as Ian's golden tongue delivered his self-promotional sales pitch that introduced me as some kind of poor relation side-kick.

During the more 'successful' business years, Ian and his brother's company moved overseas for tax purposes. While Ian stayed in the UK to continue networking and sourcing suitable clients, Paul, and his wife Iris, moved abroad. However, Ian used this as an excuse to expand his expenditure with increased overseas travel, which eventually led to the decision for the need to have an overseas rental property for when he visited. Not only did he want to have the same luxuries as Paul, such as an overseas pad; but Ian preferred this option as it would allow him to correctly store his huge collection of handmade clothing and shoes, which again, was all about promoting the image of financial success in London and abroad.

Consequently, in addition to Ian's regular trips to London, he also often went abroad, taking his mother Beryl, to visit Paul and Iris. I was unable to go as I couldn't take Lauren out of school. However, if Lauren was visiting Mac, I was on a number of occasions, able to travel with Ian, which of course, was wonderful; I love to travel and for many years, it was an unfulfilled dream.

Ian always flew first or business class, whenever he went to visit Paul overseas. When I travelled, he would book me a second class ticket, so that we sat separately. His attitude was that he couldn't put himself through travelling 'cattle class', as he called it, but I could, as my background made me more accustomed to it. It would irritate him that it really didn't bother me how I travelled. I had grown up never leaving my hometown, and with Hugh and Mac, hadn't travelled as much as I would have liked. Therefore, a flight to anywhere was always an adventure; a chance to visit a place I'd never been.

Once more, travel allowed Ian to use it as a kind of reward system. He would sometimes allow me to travel alongside him; the impetus being that it was my gift for being a 'good girl' and a reminder of how lucky I was. It was never a case of, we are couple, and we simply want to be seated together. It was always a game of sometimes you win and sometimes you lose. Except, when he thought I was losing, which was to be seated in second class, I was actually happy, because I could be at ease and not feel as though I had to pretend to be something I was not.

For me, sitting in business class felt as uneasy as eating in a five-star restaurant. And that isn't because I dislike either, or feel like I don't belong, it was because of Ian's pressure and suggestion that I didn't know how to belong in these environments that created the anxiety.

I was constantly in a position of being compared to someone else, Eva and Noelia, and being reminded that I lacked finesse, education, basic communication, and social skills; as a result, it was really easy to believe that I didn't belong in these surroundings. Likewise, it was easy to forget who I once was, which isn't to say that I was used to eating in luxury establishments, but I did have a level of confidence, ambition, and drive, that had given me hope and allowed me to dream and to believe in myself. I'd pushed myself hard to rise up in my media career, where I was accustomed, as a news desk secretary who later became a studio director, to meeting and conversing with a wide range of interesting people, from members of the public to dignitaries, from victims of crime to celebrities.

I believe that Ian's need for admiration and thriving on grandiose ideas spanned decades. He had told me the numerous stories about going to the best schools, doing the best jobs, having women chasing him and being offered the $1million to have sex; however, he had one particular narrative that placed him in his twenties, which highlighted that his taste for lavish things had been a characteristic for decades.

The infamous narrative was how Ian had earned the title of Lord. He had been visiting London on a business trip and entertaining a client in one of the city's prestigious hotel restaurants. The client had departed, and Ian had retired to the 'smoking lounge' for a cigar and cognac. It was here that he realised that he had forgotten his wallet. In a panic he called his friend to ask for help. After the phone call, the friend called the hotel and asked to speak to Lord Rodgers, referring to Ian's surname. The friend told the concierge that he was the Lord's private secretary and that he needed to speak to him urgently but believed he may have left his phone in his hotel room. He went as far as surmising that the Lord would have retired to the smoking lounge. A call was transferred to the lounge and the recipient declared to everyone within that room that there was a telephone call for Lord Rodgers.

Of course, everyone looked toward Ian, Lord Rodgers. I don't doubt that the establishment was often frequented by people with titles, so perhaps some were privately exclaiming that they hadn't heard of this particular Lord. This event happened pre Google and easy access to researching information on the Internet or mobile phones. Lord Rodgers was able to explain his predicament and the hotel decided that it would be their pleasure to allow the evening expense, without being challenged, to be on the house.

Needless to say, Ian was in his element that such a fuss was made over him due to his grand title and how it had earned him a free business meal and drinks, including the cigar and cognac. The experience fuelled his sense of grandeur and self-importance. He felt good that he had been able to pull it off and boasted to me that he had taken advantage of the title on many occasions, to the point that, Lord Rodgers became well-known on the London scene. It didn't seem to matter to him that it was based on lies and falsities.

It was important to Ian to celebrate his milestone birthdays lavishly, which would be an all-inclusive weekend hotel break for family and friends. At home, Ian and I always slept in separate bedrooms, which did extend to hotel breaks or staying with friends.

On these special birthday occasions, Ian would book a suite, where he would sleep in the master bedroom while I slept on the day bed. Again, Ian's attitude was that he needed luxury and I was used to less. Once more, while his comments could be hurtful and would leave me feeling upset, I would console myself in the fact that I was getting to stay in lovely hotels, that were always beyond my wildest dreams.

But what happened over a period of time, is that I got so used to being referred to and treated in this way, that I ended up normalising this behaviour to the point that I almost invited him to disregard me in this manner. Therefore, when it came to being invited to travel with him on an overseas business trip, I would actively volunteer for myself to travel separately or to have a lower grade room. I did this because I truly believed that I somehow deserved less, even though in my opinion, I wasn't getting less because it still felt like a treat.

Therefore, anything regarding myself would be something that would immediately be forfeited, including the celebration of my own milestone birthdays. Parties would be discouraged by Ian and referred to as an unnecessary expense. He applied the same philosophy for me organising our wedding day. Naturally, I agreed with him because beneath the surface I was highly stressed about his growing rate of expenditure. The 'successful' business years were good but not to the extent that he was spending. Therefore, I couldn't justify deepening the worry or growing debt for the sake of spending money on my own fantasy birthday party or wedding day. I was also accustomed to the cycle of accepting 'less' because 'less' never seemed so bad compared to what I had been used to.

Nonetheless, I would always find an alternative way to celebrate by organising dinner or a small party with friends. I would cook, and the wine would flow, and we would eat, good, home-cooked food and I would buy a posh dessert from somewhere like Waitrose. It was enough, because this was the truer version of me.

My childhood obviously played a huge role in shaping who I became in adulthood. After my mum left my dad for another man, my dad remarried. My stepmother was incredibly cruel to the point that I had to earn food by doing chores that were lengthy and difficult for someone of my age at that time. Lighting the fire before leaving for school would earn me a flask of orange cordial and two slices of bread and butter. Dusting the house earned me dinner, which I would eat alone in my bedroom. Sometimes, when they treated themselves to a takeaway, I was allowed to eat their leftovers. If they ate fish and chips, I thought nothing of eating just the fish skin, which I came to learn was a treat; all I saw was that I was being offered a place at their table.

Therefore, my boundaries regarding how Ian treated me was completely warped. As a result, my subservience further fuelled his narcissistic tendencies to be able to control and manipulate me via his form of reward system; if I was a 'good girl' and in favour with him, he would treat me to a better room or a first class ticket. Thus, to have the real deal, for me, was like being offered the meaty side of the fish rather than the skin or to have ham and cheese, like my siblings, inside of my sandwich. The freedom to organise my own dinner event or parties was the equivalent of eating an entire banquet of fish and chips.

I've absolutely no doubt that if Ian ever knew that I had made these accusations about him, that he would venomously defend himself and probably claim that I was extremely ungrateful for everything he has ever done for me. But my own upbringing, for which he was fully aware, I was accustomed to normalising bad behaviour or mistreatment, which in my childhood years, had also been physical.

Therefore, any behaviour that wasn't bodily harmful in my later years, was always going to feel much more wonderful than what I had got used to, which made it easy to allow the silent abuse to go undetected. According to both Walt and Maria, the emotional damage caused to me by my childhood, made me the perfect victim for someone with a narcissistic personality; my boundaries were broken, my survival mechanism was subservient people-pleaser.

Sadly, I believe that I got used to being bought, and I do feel a sense of shame about that still. I never asked Ian to buy me anything, but like a child, I would try to win his affection and in doing so, I would be rewarded with a gift. It wasn't so much that I wanted the actual gift, which invariably would be something he had bought for Eva, but it was the need to believe that the gift equalled that he loved me. And like the flight ticket, and hotel room, the gift would be something amazing and difficult to dislike. But the more I've come to know myself and to love myself in the aftermath of that relationship, those gifts are no reflection of the real me.

For a man who hated people and parties, he liked to host them during the more successful years. It was an opportunity to show guests around his Hampshire pad, filled with artwork, and a baby grand piano that no one could play. He pretended that the house belonged to us, as did the furnishings, yet most of it was purchased on credit. Guests would be wowed, drink bubbly, and listen as Ian spoke about Eva's expert knowledge on champagne; the usual patter, that led to him explaining how he had ended up with me. I was part of some kind of double-act that I never signed up to be part of. In gratitude for finding his soulmate, me apparently, he would further impress our guests by offering me an extravagant gift; including the baby grand, which I never got to play because lessons weren't a priority, I couldn't afford them. It was all just for show.

However, the more Ian's outlandish behaviour grew, the more I became irrelevant, because we would be surrounded by people who wanted to basically hang out with us in our secretly fake life; they fuelled his ego, admiring him for the grand lifestyle he had acquired.

But the performance hid the more painful detail such as I needed dental care, but he complained about the cost and so, I put the treatment on hold; I spent an entire Easter weekend in agony with a severe toothache, while entertaining guests. Likewise, stress was causing me to comfort eat. Due to weight gain, I needed a new winter coat. I told Ian that I needed one because I didn't own one that fitted. He had recently given me a lavish gift of perfume, a litre bottle of Eva's favourite, which was presented in front of house guests. So, his response was to tell me that I'd had enough; the answer to having a new coat, was no.

The following day, Ian travelled into London with his son Ollie, and bought him a coat from Jermyn Street.

During these lavish periods, I made friends with Jilly, who herself, would admit that she came from money. Her parents are wealthy. Her life always sounded like one constant big holiday. Her main issues in life seemed to evolve around what colour ski jacket to buy for the annual skiing holiday, which involved staying at the chalet she owned with her husband Nigel.

I met Jilly at the gym. She would turn up for a spin class wearing an entirely colour co-ordinated outfit, freshly painted nails, and a large diamond ring. She had a choice of Range Rovers to drive and thought nothing of spending over £100 on a single piece of underwear. What I liked about her, is that she knows who she is and makes no apology for it. She is also one of the most kind and generous people I know. She recognises that she is more fortunate than most and tries to discreetly help when she can. Her friendship has been constant regardless of how much or little I've had in my life.

Interestingly, Jilly and her husband Nigel, once offered me the opportunity to leave Ian and to stay with them until I got back on my own feet. At the time, I still believed that I would spend the rest of my life with Ian and that I was in love. Therefore, the suggestion of leaving him really upset me and I couldn't understand why Jilly and Nigel felt it necessary to make the offer, especially when I'd only ever portrayed myself as being totally happy in my marriage.

Jilly had started the conversation tentatively, knowing full well that it would upset me. But she explained that her and Nigel were worried about me. They'd got to know Ian over a number of years, and they felt that on listening to his stories, that nothing stacked up and it concerned them. They were used to being with people with money, they knew some of the top professionals working as traders and investors; whatever Ian had told them, hadn't resonated with the world that was familiar to them. They could see that I'd been totally taken in by him and that he was leading us toward an eventual train crash.

But I refused their offer to stay with them because I was too accustomed to Ian saying that most people were unlike him; I believed him when he said that due to his background in covert work that he'd been introduced to a trading world that most people didn't know existed. This meant that if he was to trade or invest, it would be at a higher level than what 'ordinary' people knew existed. I didn't see the red flag.

However, it wasn't long until the train crash began to hurtle towards its demise. Dividends due to investors, from which Ian and Paul earned commission, stopped being paid by a trader based in mainland Europe. Then began a series of excuses as to why the funds weren't being paid. Therefore, unexpectedly, Ian's paydays stopped, and he had rental properties in two other countries, and financial commitments, but had failed to save sufficient funds to support us in the case of an emergency. My money, which was used to pay the Devon mortgage had long run out and I'd started to run up secondary debts to stay afloat.

We waited months for news on what was happening with the payment of the dividends; Ian was reluctant to give up his fake Hampshire pad and to return to Devon. It was a tense time; the longer we waited the more we ran out of money, which meant that eventually we wouldn't be able to meet the cost of the mortgage, which was our main home and base. The parties stopped and soon there was hardly any visitors, apart from the few friends who stayed loyal regardless of where we lived and what we owned.

Ian hung on to the lavish lifestyle image for as long as he could. He began to sell his cars and the art to pay the rent; money that could have been more sensibly put to good use to create savings and to secure the home in Devon, but he was adamant that the trade issue would be resolved. But I'd seen it all before and any courage I found to suggest that we should decamp and return to Devon to live a more frugal life, would be shot down in flames. I also offered to return to work but again, I would be told that I could never earn enough money to get us out of the mess that had been created. He also claimed that the cost of running a vehicle to take a job would negate the money I was capable of earning.

I continued to use my writing as a form of escapism; I was still interested in esoteric subjects and this formed part of the scripts I started to write. Ian escaped into watching TV and became hooked on supernatural programmes. In an odd synchronistic way, while we were waiting for our lives to be derailed, we found a connection talking about my interest in spirituality and his avid curiosity regarding the paranormal. His enthusiasm inspired my writing, but what I didn't realise until much later, is how much he manipulated the content of my work. My original supernatural script concept was very gentle and soft. However, with Ian's encouragement, my work morphed into something much darker and demonic in nature. My old media friend and acquaintance, Hazel, loved to read my work but as my work began to change, she always stated that she hated the direction that my writing had gone.

Nonetheless, escaping into my writing did little to mask the fact that I was also living in fear of what was going to happen to us if we didn't move back to Devon. Therefore, I was already in a fearful phase, but was also having Ian fill my mind with some pretty dark stuff, which began to reflect in my writing. I loved reading books about angels, or anything that gave a deeper insight into Christ consciousness and Ian wasn't as much challenging these beliefs, but almost offering what he saw as a more equalised conversation to acknowledge the light and dark.

He convinced me that writing something more balanced would show a deeper understanding of this world rather than to offer work that was nothing but fluff. I listened to his viewpoint and started to write a very dark supernatural script. Any time we spent together we would always talk about this subject. I would often take a break from my work to ask him a question about demonic possession or seek technical jargon on how paranormal investigators would detect the energy. I could easily have researched for answers on the Internet, but I wanted to engage with Ian, to find a mutual interest and to be relevant to him.

I was also concerned about his stress levels due to the business issues and so I felt, that finding mutual ground would act as a distraction for him. But instead, it fuelled what I can only refer to as a darkness; the entire energy within our home completely changed. I was convinced that the change of atmosphere was in relation to Ian's stress and my growing fear of what would happen if he insisted on continuing to hang onto the Hampshire lifestyle.

However, it all got very bizarre and one evening while I was cooking dinner, I was convinced that I saw a man standing in the kitchen with me. It really scared me, and I went to tell Ian, who was watching TV in a different room. However, before I could speak, I realised that he was watching a supernatural programme about demonic possession and the man who was allegedly possessed, was the image I'd seen standing in the kitchen. I was speechless. I couldn't understand what had just happened.

For days after seeing the figure in the kitchen, I had the worst nightmares and I a voice telling me to end my life, which sounds horrendously dangerous. This wasn't me, no matter how bad life gets, this is not something I would do; my connection with God, as I referred to Him then, was too strong and I always believed deep down inside that I would be alright. Plus, I couldn't do that to Lauren or Hugh, who would have done anything to have lived longer, it would haven't sat right with me on any level of my spiritual beliefs.

I wanted to know whether Ian was having similar experiences. Tentatively, I asked Ian how he was feeling and as always, I shared too much about myself. He claimed that he'd also heard a voice telling him to end his life too; I wonder if he would have shared this if I had stayed silent? But instead of consoling me and discussing what should be done to get us both out of this dark space, he told me that it was my fault; that my dark moods, combined with what I was writing had invited a demonic entity to into our home.

I was flabbergasted. I knew that I could feel down, but in the main this was only because of the severe financial situation we were in. My mother had suffered from depression, and I knew what it looked like; I wasn't her, but Ian seemed insistent that I wasn't aware of my dark moods and how this attracted dark stuff into our lives.

This was dangerously harmful talk. I tried to defend myself and to tell him that I only wrote about the dark supernatural stuff because it was something we could share; I explained that I'd learnt about this material from him and asked him how he could be certain that it was I who had brought such darkness to the house. The very question made him look at me in a way that was dark in itself; he told me that I was unstable like my mother, and asked me how it could possibly be him, because he was the stable one. It was only in my stability and trust in my faith that I didn't allow Ian to drive me down to whatever level he was attempting. I cannot begin to imagine the damage he could have done if I'd genuinely suffered from mental ill health issues.

A few days after we'd both seemingly heard the demonic voice telling us to end our lives, Anita was invited to cleanse our home. At the time, Ian's mum was staying with us. Anita brought a table for table-tipping, a seemingly well-known tool for connecting with the spirit world. We sat for what felt like ages waiting for something to happen; I had a fit of the nervous giggles listening to Anita inviting whatever was within our home to speak to us. My snickering soon came to an abrupt end when the table began to move almost violently between the four of us; I couldn't believe what I was seeing. I kept looking to see who was moving the table, but there was no obvious culprit.

As the table crashed about, Anita appeared to be out of her depth, at a loss on what to say and how to manage the situation, and so Ian took over; he started to shout words about God and the mighty Archangel Michael banishing whatever entity that was around us from our home. It was all very surreal. Seemingly, Ian had become some kind of self-taught demon hunter from watching TV. It sounds almost farcical and if there was no relevance to sharing this unbelievable part of Ian's abuse, I would have eliminated it. But sadly, it did become very relevant some years later; it continues, even as I write.

Nonetheless, this initial episode marked the extent that Ian would go to play mind games, by attempting to instil fear that put into question my spiritual beliefs. He'd even played out the role of protector, which fuelled his ego and the grand idea that he was powerful enough to go into battle with a demon.

Inevitably, the trade situation never got sorted and it began to stir a hornets nest; it was the same trouble that prompted Ian's decision to later escape to Spain. Thus eventually, even he realised that it was time to decamp and return to Devon; this included having to close down the other rental properties he had acquired overseas. He refused to sell the furnishings of the Hampshire house and instead insisted on paying for storage, adamant that one day he would get it all back, bigger and better.

The storage units were crammed with belongings until months later the cost of them was no longer viable and we had to stand and observe as various local charity shops came to pick through what could be taken and the rest went to strangers or the tip. The items had no value, it was just stuff, but observing our life, and specifically Ian's dreams go up in flames was difficult. I still loved this man regardless of his flaws, but at this time, I was still unaware that our marriage was seriously unhealthy.

I found the return to Devon a blessing. There was very little to dislike about living in a house with sea views and an amazing nearby parkland. Plus, the house was cosy; it was more self-contained, which meant that if we were to get financially back on track, we could feasibly focus on creating a 'home'. I'd made a few friends in the southwest over the years and so it enabled us to reconnect too.

I cautiously returned to writing but stayed clear of creating dark supernatural content. I still wanted to engage with Ian and to find a common ground for us to connect; this felt even more important after leaving Hampshire, because his mood was low, and I'd seen how allowing his input into my work had been a distraction for him.

As a result, I ended up writing about Ian's life, telling the story of his 'covert' military work. What I didn't realise at the time, is that it allowed him once more, to be centre of attention and to share his personal grandiose ideas while permitting me to write. Because the focus was now on him and not a demonic entity, it allowed his ego to be fuelled in the process. Therefore, he was bound to be very supportive of me writing books and filmscripts that placed him as the heroic protagonist.

He would record his story onto a cassette tape, and I would transcribe his words into a book or script format. The lines between fantasy, fiction and factual often became somewhat blurred to the point that even though I had volunteered to be in this writing process, I was left wondering what parts of his story were real. He would use the opportunity to further distil my feelings of inadequacy, with supposed tales of his 007-style work involving lots of women lusting for him. He stated that the bigger the gun, the more women would chase after him. Part of the fantasy was gorgeous big-breasted twins fighting over him and having to satisfy both at the same time, which admittedly, I guess isn't just the whims of someone with narcissistic traits.

But what makes it continue to be covertly abusive, is the constant regularity of finding and using every opportunity, to twist the scenario into a method of control and manipulation. As a result, I was inadvertently feeding his egotistic self and creating a monster in the process of finding a way to distract him from what he had lost and to fulfil my own needs guilt-free.

And while, I think it's wonderful to have ambition and to have dreams and I would encourage anyone to chase them. But what I was allowing was someone else to control my dreams. In fuelling his ego, I allowed him to deepen his overall control and manipulation toward me.

Nonetheless, once Ian had found his feet again, he began to return to London in the hope of finding new business opportunities; he was always reluctant to accept that he could perhaps find what he sought closer to home. He would return home from his business trips claiming that he had been in talks with potential literary agents and discussions regarding film financing, which then fuelled my ego into believing that I could become a successful writer.

Like his grandiose ideas to one-day be a millionaire: billionaire as the years passed; I was buying into the idea that I was going to be this amazing scriptwriter and that my work was going to be in demand. We even had conversations about which Hollywood director we would want, and which actor would play Ian; what beautiful actresses would play his love-interests.

This led me to processing the belief that if I could find my purpose, and this enabled me to have financial worth, then I could make Ian like me more. The put-downs and third-party referrals had worsened since our return to Devon; which made it all the more difficult to listen to the recordings I transcribed, that were like listening to his sexual fantasy pods. Yet, the reality was that I'd literally handed him the carrot to dangle in-front of me and I followed like a total ass believing that one day that I would reach it.

My belief in him, my love, my trust, and the fact that I'd placed him on a pedestal, meant that he could use my dreams in a narrative that basically encouraged me to normalise his grandiose ideas, while he took complete control as the one making the contacts to promote *my work;* in doing so it allowed him to talk about himself. It was him, not me, who was visiting London where he had seemingly made literary and film contacts. Meanwhile, he was actively discouraging me from reaching out myself as he claimed that only he knew the people that mattered; the ones with money: not the monkeys but the organ-grinders as he put it.

Notably, this 'writing' venture, continued for fifteen of the twenty years we were together. It became just another topic of conversation like Eva, whereby Ian could share stories about how his life was so interesting that it had stirred attention from agents and film financiers. And yet, not once did he read any of my work; he claimed that he hated reading and boasted that he had never read a book in his life. He had no interest in what I was doing, and because of my own insecurities, I would naturally question whether my work was good enough to put in-front of the important contacts he claimed to be making.

His attitude was that money talked: he basically told me that even if my work was shit, if there was enough money behind it, it would get made regardless of whether I had talent or not. While I think there is an overall element of truth in this statement, it nonetheless, was just another example of Ian making me believe that I needed him to become anything of remote value, that I needed him to exist.

When I eventually did leave Ian, I destroyed everything that I'd ever written; I deleted 20 years of work. Interestingly, when I told a fellow writing friend the truth about my life with Ian, they told me that they'd always wondered why I never did anything to progress my work; I never pushed it to further my writing career.

Likewise, even though I walked away from Ian, the damage that the relationship has done to my mental well-being runs very deep. I have moments of believing that I'll sink and cannot survive without him. At times I wonder whether I'll discover the darkness that he says is part of my genes; that my conversations with my Holy Father are indeed a sign of the alleged inherited madness. I consider most days, whether I am good enough.

> *"Throughout most of our history, nothing — not flood, famine, plague, or new weapons has endangered humanity one-tenth as much as the narcissistic ego, with its self-aggrandizing presumptions and its hell-hound spawn of*
> *fear and greed."*

[Source: Tom Robbins]

5

Red Flag: Manipulation

Narcissists are skilled manipulators, deftly twisting situations to their benefit. They masterfully employ a range of emotional tools, including charm, guilt, fear, and more to control individuals and outcomes. In a work context, a narcissist colleague might use charm to gain favour with superiors. In a family dynamic, they might leverage guilt to maintain control. Family members may feel obliged to meet their demands because 'family owes each other.' They create an atmosphere of fear or tension that discourages family members from challenging their behaviour.

In a romantic relationship, the narcissist often manipulates their partners to keep them off-balance: showering their partner with affection one moment, then withdrawing the next, to create a sense of insecurity. They are likely to provoke jealousy to sow doubt and ensure their partner is continually striving for their approval.

Again, all red flags in narcissistic abuse are forms of manipulation. Manipulation can be defined as controlling someone or something to your own advantage, often unfairly or dishonestly.

During my 20-year relationship with Ian, he would be the one who decided when I should be a stay at home wife or mother and when I was to seek employment. Hunting for a job would always coincide with the periods that his business was struggling financially. It galled him to admit that his own ventures were failing, and he would invariably blame everyone else but himself whenever there were any business problems. Generally, he disliked me going to work and would actively discourage me from having a career. But when we needed the money, he permitted it, while still ensuring that I was aware that whatever I was capable of earning was meagre in comparison to his own potential. It was important to him that I never got too confident, because if I did, there was the risk that I would no longer believe that I needed him. To instil this, he often belittled my employment role and claimed that my low salary was due to lack of education and abilities.

Additionally, whenever I was required to work, childminding was also a big issue, which I recognise is a problem for lots of parents. The kind of employment that I was able to get, never paid enough to meet the cost of living and childcare. As a result, I could only go to work if the role was part-time or if Ian was willing to help care for Lauren, which was something he swore was never to be his responsibility. Hence, we really did need to hit hard times for Ian to agree to me returning to work.

When I did return to full-time work, this would always place added pressure on me, as I would then try to overcompensate for Ian taking care of Lauren by taking on additional duties so that he didn't have to do them. Due to lack of funds, Ian was unable to travel to London to instigate business openings, which meant that he was at home all day. However, in an attempt to keep the situation calm, I would prep meals in advance, pack Lauren's school lunch, and still do all of the washing and ironing.

I loved going to work, it gave me purpose and allowed me to meet other people outside of my home environment. However, I always felt that I should never appear to enjoy my job, as I feared that this would suggest to Ian that I preferred work to being a wife and mother. Sometimes, I wanted to talk about my day at work, but it was never of any interest to him. I guess a part of me wanted to share my 'small work achievements' in an attempt to highlight the positive traits that other people, employers, saw in me.

Nonetheless, any aspirations to get ahead in whatever job role I was doing at the time, would be discouraged because career advancement potentially would steal too much of my time, and in Ian's opinion the pay would never be worth the extra work hours required to progress. If he detected that I was upset by the dissuasion, he would remind me that I had parental duties or if he felt inclined, would resort to convincing me that I didn't have the correct mindset; he would undermine my mental stability to take on additional pressure in my place of work. And, because I believed in the many flaws Ian saw in me, I too would begin to question whether I had the required abilities to dream a little bigger.

One day, I saw a very rare opportunity to work in media based in Devon. The job was absolute gold dust; and I truly believe that if the same post had been advertised in London, my application would have gone straight into the waste bin. However, the job was local, so I calculated that there wouldn't be many people with my media industry skillset, albeit a little rusty, living in the southwest.

My media career was an area of my life that Ian hadn't been part of, except from the initial period when we had first met. As a result, this meant that this was a world that he knew nothing about, and had therefore, not had the opportunity to discredit any achievements I'd made in this field. Consequently, there was a part of me that Ian hadn't been able to destabilise, which allowed me to still hold onto knowing my strengths in this field of work.

So, I applied for the position and my application was successful. The pay was really good compared to the numerous available temping roles I'd previously undertaken; the only downside was the location, which required a 70 mile round trip. In the past I'd travelled further for work, but I knew that Ian would calculate earnings against mileage and wear and tear on the vehicle. My mode of transport was Eva's car, a bright yellow Megane.

The other downside of the media job was the erratic hours that I would be required to work. I was returning to working in a newsroom, which entailed almost 24/7 coverage. But I really wanted the job. I missed the buzz of working in media and while the position was a temporary contract, I felt that it was a second chance to build the career I'd always wanted. But to do so, I would have to pay a big price in ensuring that I did everything I could to keep Ian calm and happy, while I returned to not just a job, but my career.

Nonetheless, even Ian knew that we needed the income and money was a language that he understood.

The long hours meant that Ian had to collect Lauren from school and make dinner for just the two of them. I would return home late at night to complaints of him feeling tired, or the silent treatment. On other occasions, if I was working an earlier shift, I would join Ian and Lauren for an evening meal. He would sometimes cook for us, and we would sit at the table to eat our meal. I enjoyed these moments, because we felt like a family and Ian was good at cooking, although he would deny this so as not to allow me to get used to the prospect. Needless to say, my work pattern created a lot of stress as I never knew what mood I would be returning home to, which then would push my people-pleaser button into overdrive: pushing me further and deeper into taking on more chores to appease Ian as much as possible.

At the same time, I was returning to a broadcast production role and technology had moved on; shifted from analogue to digital. While I had previously been accustomed to a multi-tasking industry, my return to work required me to take on even more duties due to more and more downsizing, which required smaller teams to deliver the same amount of content. As a result, I had to learn new skills to advance and to stay up-to-date within the industry. Because I had an excellent track record in media production, time was invested in my training regardless of the role being temporary; the long-term plan was that with my skills updated, I could potentially cover staff shortages on a freelance basis.

However, trying to balance work and home life, I soon began to feel as though I was burning the candle at both ends. I really wanted the opportunity to return to a media career, but I just wasn't getting the support I needed from Ian to enable me to ease myself slowly back into the high pressure of working in a live news environment, with home and family. I was earning good money, and it helped us a lot. But instead of support, I was met with Ian's irrational moods.

I recognise that it is common for anyone who is trying to juggle work, home, and family to be met with relationship challenges. However, in a healthy relationship, both parties will discuss and work toward solving the problem so that they can find peace and harmony to reinstate their loving union. But in a narcissistic partnership, the union is not based on love, but on control and manipulation, which means that their needs will always be priority regardless of whether it is detrimental to the other person. Thus, instead of finding a loving and harmonious solution, I continued to overcompensate, and to try to relieve Ian from as many excessive duties as possible.

It was only a matter of time before I would burn out. I was severely torn because I wanted my job and to earn a wage, so that I could contribute to supporting my family. Yet, my stress levels were at an all-time high due to juggling too many obligations and this was heightened also by the fear of failure. I didn't want to give Ian any more ammunition to compare me to Eva, or to continue to question my mental stability, or to give him something else to add to my already over extended list of flaws. So, when it all got too much, I began to experience severe and debilitating panic attacks.

The first panic attack came out of the blue, as they do. I was working a late news shift. We had been running a story about a rescued injured deer; the news item included a shot of the wounded animal, with a small amount of blood around its mouth. The news story had a happy ending and was run several times throughout the day, which meant that I had viewed the footage several times.

As my shift continued toward midnight, I could feel my anxiety about working late and Ian's subsequent bad mood increasing. During the rehearsal for the late night news bulletin, the rescued deer story was included in the line-up as it made the perfect happy-ending story. However, on watching the footage, the sight of the deer's blood unexpectedly triggered a memory flash of Hugh's dead body. I've no idea to this day, how my mind linked the deer story to Hugh, but it did, and that one prompt was to have a devastating effect on my life.

At the time, I didn't know what was happening to me. I suddenly felt very stressed and panicked. My heart was one minute racing with fear and then suddenly, I was plunged into a sensation that felt like a cold numbness, as if I was falling into an abyss. My body had seemingly gone into fight or flight mode, and it had uncontrollably opted for flight, resulting in part shutdown, which made me feel woozy; I thought I was going to faint. It was a battle to stay conscious and to get through the live news bulletin.

The late bulletin was broadcast without any obvious technical issues, but while directing, I had to repeatedly sing *Ten Green Bottles* to myself as a distraction. After we came off air, I didn't mention the experience to anyone, as the likelihood was that it was a one-off and I didn't want to risk losing my job.

However, it wasn't a limited incident, the problem escalated very quickly and soon became out of control. After the initial attack, I began to worry as to whether it would happen again. I started to question whether after a six-year break from the industry, I'd lost my confidence to work in live broadcasting and if I was still good enough to have a career in this field.

I was unable to turn to Ian for support because again I felt that this would prove him right regarding my mental instability and overall ability to do anything well. I soon spiralled into a chicken-and-egg kind of scenario; stressing whether I would have another panic attack at work became increasingly conducive to one occurring.

The attacks quickly mushroomed out of control. At first, I was fine working in the newsroom, but as soon as it was time to go into the gallery for the live broadcasts, the panic would start: the gallery seemed to be a trigger, because this is where the first attack occurred. I would then worry about my next shift for hours in advance; this then turned to feeling anxious a day and then days before my next scheduled live broadcast. I multi-tasked so not all shifts involved live programmes.

This then escalated from the newsroom into the car, so that travelling to work became problematic regardless of what newsroom role I was scheduled. Driving to work became hellish; I would sing or listen to loud music for the entire journey, terrified that the sensations I was experiencing would end in fainting. If I fainted, I thought about how I could potentially kill others as well as myself. My thought process was not rational. I knew that I could drive and that I wasn't scared of driving, but I was scared of fainting due to the high anxiety.

I functioned like this for three years. At no point was I ever able to rationalise the fact that I successfully was able to do my job and drove to work without fainting; time didn't heal in this process. It was years of high anxiety, worrying about driving to and from work, hours, days, or a week in advance. It was pulling over into laybys where I would sit and cry until I could get my head together again. It was sleepless nights and keeping up with my profession in an ever changing industry, while allowing the people-pleaser side of me, to continually overcompensate at home.

I stopped offering to drive whenever I was in the car with Ian; he preferred to drive, but often he would take us on long road trips and need me to drive when he tired. I would feign headaches and illness so that he wouldn't ask me to take over the steering wheel; this then made it appear that I was constantly ill, which again added to the list of my many failings.

At the same time, I continued to be subjected to Ian's psychological abuse, the third-party referrals, the comparisons, and the silent treatment. I was also comfort eating, and my eczema was bad, and all of this added to my feelings of inferiority. The whole time I was thinking that this was my own doing because I believed that I was everything that Ian had led me to believe I was, which was that I wasn't good enough and that I needed to work on improving myself. As a result, I was permanently on edge and new triggers were regularly emerging that would cause panic attacks in unexpected scenarios. Nowhere felt safe.

One evening while Ian was away in London and Lauren was visiting Mac in Yorkshire, I decided to go to see a play at the local theatre; the production, *The Vagina Monologues*, was being presented by a touring company. Unlike Ian, I loved going to the theatre and in an ideal world, I would love to go and see a play or show every week. Therefore, with my family away, it felt like a wonderful opportunity to do something that I really enjoyed.

However, for the first 30 minutes of the performance I didn't hear a single word. The production was a sell-out and therefore, the theatre was full; it felt crammed. I was sat in the middle of a row, with people sat all around me. I felt hemmed in and all I could think about was what would happen if I fainted; I thought about how my fat carcass would be removed from the theatre. I imagined the local news headline: *Fat Woman Faints Bringing Famous Play to a Halt*. My concerns weren't vanity based, but bore from a place of shame, self-disgust, and fear; the years of insults and painful neglect had led me to seeing myself as one of life's hideous burdens.

So, for the first 30 minutes of the show, I repeatedly sang *Ten Green Bottles* to myself. Eventually, I calmed down and really enjoyed the performance. But what should have been a wonderful treat to me, turned into a nightmare. Even now, on the rare occasions I get to go to the theatre, I have to book an aisle seat; I need to know that I can escape. I need a clear runway for flight mode.

Naturally, I tried to avoid anything that could trigger an episode. However, as the problem escalated it became impossible to safeguard against having an attack, because new triggers and scenarios kept emerging.

One day, I was food shopping at the supermarket when I saw a man with a bandage and patch covering one of his eyes. My mind went into overdrive, and this triggered my anxiety. I saw flashes of Hugh's dead body, the detail of his mottled purple skin. I recollected my visits to him at the chapel of rest and how his face appeared distorted and how, when touching his chest, it felt as though it had been stuffed with newspapers.

As before, my heart began to race and moments later, I felt a sudden cold numbness and sinking feeling. The supermarket aisles began to spin. I had the same overwhelming irrational fear of fainting and the humiliation that would cause. I thought about Ian who was waiting in the car and the added disgrace that would cause if he had to come and get me, which made the entire experience feel worse. I sang to myself while erratically piling things into my shopping trolley as a form of distraction. Eventually, I calmed down and got through the episode without fainting. However, the supermarket became a new trigger for me.

Finally admitting the problem to Ian came during a day trip to the beautiful coastal town of Sidmouth, in South Devon; I guess you could say that it was more a reveal than a confession. I saw a man in a wheelchair, both of his legs had been amputated. On this occasion, the panic attack came without any warning: I didn't feel the familiar sensation of wooziness or a racing heart. I went into total meltdown without the opportunity to internally rationalise; to talk myself down from the edge.

One second, I was walking along the street, talking to Lauren and Ian about buying an ice-cream; I saw the man and seconds later I went into what felt like a semi-conscious state. In my mind there was a frozen image of the man's amputated legs with flashes of Hugh's dead body. I began to mumble the song, *Ten Green Bottles* to myself; I was vaguely aware that I was singing more audibly than normal, which drew attention from Ian, Lauren, and passers-by.

I was also aware that I began to tap my right thigh with my fingers and that I started to spin around in circles while chuntering the song. I recall how terrified Lauren looked, observing my odd behaviour, but I wasn't able to stop. After that, everything is a blur. I was told that I didn't faint, but I have absolutely no recollection on how I managed to make it to a nearby hotel. I seem to have only gained full consciousness once seated in the hotel and was drinking warm sugary tea.

Both Ian and Lauren were clearly shaken by the experience. I promised Lauren that I was okay and that I just hadn't felt very well. Later, when Lauren was in bed, I spoke to Ian about the incident. I admitted that I'd been struggling with panic attacks for over three years. I didn't tell him about the pressure I felt juggling my career with responsibilities at home; I didn't want to appear weak or incapable.

Instead, I focused on telling him about the deer story and how it had acted as an odd trigger; I omitted the part about how it was affecting my entire work life. But I did admit to the fact that my driving had been severely affected by the problem. I explained that I felt that it possibly stemmed from unresolved issues relating to Hugh's death; I felt inclined to remind Ian that I had woken up next to a dead body, which would potentially traumatise the strongest of people.

I knew that Ian didn't do sympathy or empathy, but I did hope that my opening up to him with a problem that had become debilitating, would elicit some level of warmth and support. Likewise, if he had kept a huge problem to himself for years, I would have been upset that he hadn't felt that he could speak to me about it. Not Ian. He had no apparent remorse or questions as to why I'd kept this difficult problem to myself.

To have been given hugs or kisses, and reassurances that I was doing an amazing job and that everything would be okay, would have gone some way to help me. But Ian was part of the problem; most of the anxiety was linked to the fear of failure and the expectation of his judgement. There was no recognition of me being emotionally, mentally, and physically burnt out. Ian's contribution to the situation was to tell me that my panic attacks made no sense. As far as he was concerned, I could drive and therefore, the solution wasn't to allow fear to get in the way, but to overcome the problem by continuing to drive. Discussion over.

I returned to the same cycle of burning the candle at both ends, organising everything, and feeling extremely hurt that my very own husband, Ian, was incapable of showing a single gram of compassion. There were no pep talks prior to driving to work to build my confidence, no words of encouragement to tell me that I was strong and capable. He would simply comment on how illogical my reaction was, which compelled me to stay silent and to bottle the problem up again.

I'm not exactly sure of the timeline between Ian becoming aware of my panic attacks and the media work eventually drying up, but it did. I can confidently say that I managed to be professional to the very end, but there were more staff cuts and pressure for the company to slash their budget. This meant that contracts weren't renewed, and freelancers were underutilised, which drove their fees to become highly competitive. A rival media company had recently closed its regional office, which resulted in more people looking for freelance work. As a result, I couldn't vie for roles against a younger, single person, who was able to locally couch hop. Additionally, it stopped being cost effective to drive a 70-mile round trip for limited hours.

While I was feeling professionally rejected, realising that this really was potentially the end of my media career forever; Ian used the event to condemn the industry to his own advantage. He told me that if I'd been of any value, I would have been offered a staff position instead of been cast aside like trash; while the statement was partially true, it was offered with a sentiment of point scoring satisfaction. It enabled him to claim that he always knew that the media industry was garbage; a declaration that felt like he needed to make a point about my incapability to have a meaningful and successful career.

Unfortunately, his sentiment cut deep, because it echoed how I felt about myself. I wanted more from the industry, and I wanted to be wanted, to regain a sense of purpose and some kind of ambition and control over my own life. But it was all too common within TV as tons of talented and gifted programme makers are cast aside every single day. I was just one of them and it meant relinquishing myself to the full force of Ian's contempt.

Thus, the fizzling out of my media career, gave Ian a kind of renewed power to be overly righteous. On the rare occasions I'd spoken of my profession, there had been this overwhelming sense that it irritated him. It didn't serve him to receive evidence that potentially disproved the way in which he labelled me wasn't true. For me to have an air of confidence brought from achieving my own career success didn't feed his overall control and manipulation agenda. But after my career ended again, Ian was able to gain pride in belittling the industry and could return to adding more negative labels to my long list of failings. I had to work harder to appease him, to win back his approval, because I believed I had failed.

To make this situation worse, he could now add to the long list of shortcomings my inability to drive. With no job, and therefore, no need to drive, Ian relished the fact that he would have to drive everywhere because I wasn't able to do so. Again, I would attempt to overcompensate and ask if that was okay with him and depending on his mood, he would switch from it not being a problem as he preferred to be the one driving or sarcastically stating,

"I don't have any choice, do I?"

Once more, I would attempt to offer an apology for my imperfections and over explain myself in the hope that I would gain some understanding. I openly shared every part of my life as a means to vindicate my behaviour and having had plenty of time to reflect on the panic attacks, I had come to realise that driving was perhaps a natural anxiety trigger for me.

In childhood, my mum's mental ill health had resulted in her threatening to commit suicide on many occasions. There were various avenues for her to take, one included the threat to jump out of a moving car. As a child, I learnt to sense my mum's moods. When needed, I would sit anxiously on the back seat behind her, watching for her to reach out toward the car door handle. When her hand went anywhere near the handle I would scream at her, begging her not to jump. My terrified screams alerted the driver to bring the car to a screeching halt.

Likewise, during my marriage to Mac, he had served in the military at a time when the IRA (Irish Republican Army) were targeting British military personnel posted to

Germany. The vehicles belonging to the military personnel and their families, had distinctive black and white numberplates, which made each and every one of the drivers and passengers a sitting target.

There were a number of horrendous shooting incidents. The military base was on high alert, and we were taught how to check our cars for bombs. I would follow procedure even late at night when all I wanted to do was get into my car and lock the doors. But during this period, the car was no longer a safe place to be; the incidents had mainly been shootings of drivers when the vehicle had come to a standstill. I would physically shake approaching every single traffic light, pleading for it to stay on green while scanning the area for any suspicious people; knowing full well that terrorists don't carry large warning signs.

Ian always hated to be couped up in the house. Wherever we lived and whatever was occurring in our lives at the time, his ideal day, would be spent driving. He could spend between 8-10 hours in the car. He usually drove in silence, while smoking a cigar and drinking a black coffee. The smell of his cigar would always linger in my hair and clothes, which I think he liked; like a cat marking its territory.

There is little to dislike about trips across Dartmoor or Exmoor; the scenery is breath-taking. But being Ian's full-time companion often felt stressful. The hours of silence were difficult to gauge hour after hour; what was allegedly his thinking time, often felt like extreme extended periods of stonewalling. If I spoke, he would often tell me to be quiet as he needed to concentrate on driving. If there was any mishap, such as skimming a hedge or missing a turn, it would be my fault for distracting him. If I tried to read, he would start talking or suddenly need me to grab the map to navigate a journey we had done a hundred times before. If I questioned this, he would claim that he wanted me to see if there was a different route If I fell asleep, he would need me to reach for his cigars or pass him some food. It was like being his full-time assistant; he clicked his fingers or pointed to what he needed, and I would get it for him.

In isolation this sounds almost petty and irrelevant. And yet, there were times that he would let me sleep in the car and I'd wake feeling guilty. I would apologise for falling asleep and depending on Ian's mood, would be either greeted with a comment that showed an element of concern; he'd left me to sleep as I was clearly tired. But more often than not, he would complain that he'd gone to the bother to take me on a road trip, and I was missing it because I was asleep. He always played a deep and twisted mind game. One that was always so discreet that it could be easily plausible. But like every part of my life with him, the long road trips were just something else that formed part of the torment.

After revealing I suffered from panic attacks, which were often triggered when driving, Ian systematically used driving to deepen my level of fear of being in a moving vehicle. He would drive at high speeds, what I would determine as dangerous, on the motorways. He would boast about his ability as an advanced driver to expertly handle the car. He went as far as claiming that he was trained in high speed getaway driving; a skill he had learnt in the military.

We would travel for hours and then he would declare that he was tired and challenge me to drive home. He knew that I couldn't and would drive more erratically to get us home quicker, while stating that tiredness at the wheel can kill. The speed and the talk of danger and death would heighten my anxiety; I would sit with my eyes closed, fighting back tears, feeling stupid for not being able to drive; for letting him down and for not being able to help out when he needed me to. But ultimately shaking with fear.

When his business entailed several trips abroad to Austria, Ian would opt to drive through France and Germany. He would drive up to 900km in a day, which he claimed would be to challenge himself. But at the same time, he would make it known to me that he needed plenty of coffee and cigars to help him stay awake. Therefore, in my role as his personal assistant, I had to ensure that he always had plenty of coffee and I was to light his cigars for him while he drove. At first, this felt cutely romantic, but as the years past, it became a gruelling psychological chore.

The night before a trip I wouldn't be able to sleep, so I would get into the car already exhausted. I would then be on watch, ensuring that Ian was constantly supplied with cigars and coffee, to ensure that he didn't fall asleep at the wheel; this meant I couldn't possibly risk falling asleep myself. I would also regularly check in on him to ask how he was feeling, internally terrified that he was annoyed that the huge task of driving had fallen on him yet again; regardless of the insane task to set a goal to drive 900km in one sitting.

When tiredness started to hit him, he would revert to talking about how fatigue kills. I would suggest that he took a break and slept, but he would refuse stating that he wanted to reach our destination. This piled more and more guilt on me for not being able to offer to drive; I would then apologise for my failings, express my upset that I was letting him down. Then in an attempt to get to our destination quicker, Ian's driving would become more and more erratic, to the point that at times I would need to close my eyes and to sit on my hands; I had to do this to stop myself from jumping out of the vehicle. I didn't want to jump from a moving car to actually kill myself, I just wanted to get away from what felt like danger.

Hence, when my anxiety was severe, it felt like I was capable of doing anything, no matter how precarious or illogical, simply to escape. Once I'd reached this state, I had to sit on my hands to stop myself from opening the car door to jump. Even as I write that sentence, I'm beginning to question whether anyone, Ian, is capable of such wicked mind games to the extent that he could push me into contemplating jumping from the vehicle; actually, playing out my own childhood nightmare regarding my mum's threats to do the same. I feel that he certainly knew that his erratic driving increased my levels of anxiety, because the conversation would always be the same.

Thus, as soon as I was in a heightened state of fear, he would always suggest that it was my turn to drive because he was too tired to continue. He knew that I would say no and therefore, we would enter into a back and forth discussion that continued along the lines of him telling me that my thought process was illogical. He would play the victim, because he had no choice but to get us to our destination. I would be reminded of the dangers of driving when excessively tired. I would apologise over and over again, then spend the rest of the journey feeling guilty and subjected to his silent treatment. It was hell.

For twelve years I didn't drive, which meant that I was totally dependent on Ian if I needed to go anywhere. Because I didn't want to upset him, I would be very cautious about requesting a lift. I would find myself invariably apologising when asking when it would be convenient to go food shopping; a task that was done for both our benefits. I learnt to manipulate him to get what I needed by offering to make him his favourite meal; it was another survival tactic. The only difference with my form of manipulation is that mine was always designed to make him feel good, unlike the form he used against me. However, whatever method I used to survive shouldn't have been needed if the relationship had been healthy.

At other times, I would need to go to the dentist or for a medical appointment and in all honesty, I can say that Ian never let me down, he took me to wherever I needed to go. But the parts that are hidden is the silent treatment when I stepped in or out of the car if he'd been kept waiting longer than he'd expected. Again, he would use the third party referral mind game, which in this scenario, he made a reference to his ex-wife Jane and told me that whenever she kept him waiting, he would drive off and leave her.

I took this story as he intended me to, that if my time in the supermarket or dentist, exceeded a normal amount of time that he would leave me too. What this did to me, for over a decade, was heighten my levels of anxiety, because I always felt rushed to complete what was needed in a minimum amount of time. I was fearful of being abandoned and more so, absolutely terrified of the aftermath.

Thus, if there were queues at the supermarket checkout or an appointment was running late, my anxiety levels would rocket. I would dash back to the car, where I would apologise over and over again; repeating the cycle of saying sorry for not being able to drive and for the fact that he had to drive me everywhere. Internally I would be pleading to hear words of comfort from him, but instead, he would tell me that he felt like a taxi driver. For me, this comment made me feel guilty and it stung to think that 'he' felt devalued in any way. This led to me never asking for a lift to a social event or to see a friend, because I didn't want him to feel undervalued. As a result, I slowly became even more isolated. The only time I got to see friends is if they arranged to come and see me, or if they were within easy walking distance.

My old friend, Hazel, from my Yorkshire media days, would drive over and stay for a few nights, several times a year. Ian would be the perfect co-host and offer to take us out for lunch. After eating, Ian would suggest that the two of us go off to take a look around the shops while he enjoyed a post meal coffee and cigar. Hazel would soon find herself caught up in the mad dash to not keep Ian waiting. I'd got used to gauging how long it took him to smoke two cigars and this was usually the cut-off point at which his irritation would set in.

Even if there were still some very alluring shops still to be explored, I'd turn back; I was too scared to keep Ian waiting.

As a result, I would hurry Hazel along and insist that we got back to Ian, and she would be irritated because she was having time away from her sons and wanted to amble along at her own leisure. One day, some years into my relationship with Ian, she warned me that my fear was an issue and as always, I protected Ian, stating that him agreeing to drive me everywhere was a sign of his love for me. Hazel claimed that it was a form of control; I ignored her advice and was in fact, quite upset with her for some time after.

Nonetheless, Hazel never mentioned it again and on following trips, would insist on taking her own car if we wanted to go out. She too seemed to know what needed to be done to appease Ian; she would make small offerings of wine or a single Cuban cigar to stay on the right side of him. She had experience of a similar relationship, and it's sad that I didn't listen to her when she recognised behavioural patterns and tried to warn me. But I'd convinced myself that deep down, love existed in the root of our relationship. I also believed that I couldn't survive without him, which I defined as evidence of how deep our love ran. As true friends go, Hazel kept on turning up and moulding herself into whatever was needed to ensure that she could continue to play a part in my life; this was her way of keeping an eye on me.

The longer Ian and I were together, it certainly felt as though the control and manipulation got worse. As he aged and his own dreams began to feel unobtainable, he seemed to have a need to up the ante to see how far he could push the boundaries. If life didn't fulfil or amuse him, he showed a need to be entertained and the only way he knew how, was to gain pleasure in luring me into a sense of safety before pulling the rug from beneath my feet.

One day we were chatting and enjoying lunch on a gloriously sunny day in Spain. I've no idea what we spoke about, but it had felt upbeat and certainly full of promise for the future. Nevertheless, this must have been a lunch date toward the end of our relationship but prior to the series of synchronicities and the very concept that I would leave Ian within the next year.

During the lunch, I remember feeling as though Ian was truly seeing and hearing me; as if there was this lingering sense that perhaps the Mediterranean had somehow warmed him too. I toyed with the idea that he was mellowing and that there was a promise of a rekindled love. I blamed myself or circumstance for everything that hadn't felt right in our relationship to date, which allowed me to believe that if everything else, but Ian changed, that our marriage could be perfect. Nonetheless, for a brief moment, I found my old self, where I shone with love and enthusiasm for a new life abroad that still had the potential to fulfil dreams, where nothing was impossible.

After the meal, Ian handed me his bank card, which bore my name, and asked me to pay the bill, while he collected the car. This was unusual for him, as he normally preferred to pay; he disliked the appearance of a woman paying the bill on his behalf. Likewise, the car was visible from the terrace where we were dining, so it seemed odd that he would choose to get the vehicle, when it was within very easy walking distance.

Inside the restaurant there was a small queue of people waiting to pay. The other diners, the owner and his wife, the chef, were all very friendly and chatted to me while I waited for my turn to pay the check. It didn't take an absurd amount of time for my turn to come around. I didn't engage in overly long conversations with anyone; I was only inside the restaurant for the length of time it took to pay. However, after I'd paid the bill, I stepped out of the restaurant to find that Ian had gone; he'd driven off without me.

My first reaction was confusion as I frantically looked for his car; I thought I must be mistaken and that he was waiting for me somewhere unexpected. But he really had gone. I then tried texting him to ask where he was; I reminded him that I was paying the bill as he'd asked me to. I didn't get a response. I then went into fear mode. I had no money on me, only Ian's bank card. It was June and the temperature was already soaring, which meant that I would have to walk without water; I would quickly dehydrate. I was also not wearing shoes suitable for the walk home. However, none of this created as much fear as getting home and being greeted by one of Ian's moods; a temper that I really didn't deserve.

Likewise, his lack of care for my safety and wellbeing struck a chord so deep down inside, I didn't think it was possible to ever heal from the pain of the level of unworthiness I was made to feel. I felt like garbage, something that could be tossed away when he got bored. It left me feeling so broken, that I truly believed that I would be beyond repair forever. Yet still, I questioned whether I had contributed to my own demise by being happy and content for a brief moment in our relationship together. I still sought to blame myself for the outcome.

I had no choice but to walk home. I did have Ian's bank card, so I re-entered the restaurant and made some light conversation about having agreed with my husband that I wanted to walk back home after the meal; I jokingly referred to my weight and said I needed the exercise to walk off the meal. I explained that I'd left my water bottle in the car and asked if I could buy a bottle; I explained that I could only pay by card because I didn't have any money on me. Thankfully, the restaurant owner just gave me a bottle of water; his kindness, almost made me burst into tears.

I walked home and I was really grateful for the water. The walk had a steep decline before an even steeper incline. I calculated that if I didn't drink until I reached the uphill part of the walk then I would stay hydrated; my philosophy appeared to work. I broke the track down into sections. Looked at where I was heading and would mentally mark out places to stop for a breather, to stand in the shade or to take a drink when the terrain got tough.

I tried to place myself in a positive mindset; to view myself as a 50-something woman on a mountain walk in Spain, looking at the most spectacular landscape. I tried telling myself I was having an adventure, but the closer I got to home, the more I wanted it all to just end. I wondered what would happen if I collapsed, had a heart attack, would he actually care. What if I was bitten by a snake or gored by wild boar, would he even miss me. My overly dramatic thoughts sound somewhat silly, but a combination of the heat and tiredness and sadness and fear, pushed me to think of irrational ways out; because I really did want out in that moment. I wanted anything, other than to face him.

By the time I reached home, I was sweating and exhausted. I had run out of water. My skin was red. My feet were sore, and I felt angry, but was too scared to fully express it. Ian was watching TV with his feet up. He didn't even look up when I entered the room. I didn't want to give him the satisfaction of having beaten me down yet again, so I casually asked him what had happened, stating I thought he was waiting for me while I paid the bill. He told me that it didn't take that long to pay a bill; he had seen me talking and so had driven off. I told him that I was only talking to people while waiting to pay the bill; he seemed nonplussed. I told him that I had tried calling him. His response was to say that his phone had been on silent. For a moment I stood in the painful silence; observed as he didn't even turn to acknowledge me. I decided to tell him that I had enjoyed my walk home but needed a rest.

I went to my bedroom and silently cried. I was mad, because I'd sworn that I would never put myself in a vulnerable position like this again with Ian. He'd driven off before during a trip to Cyprus and as a result, I'd promised that I would never allow myself to be open to such vulnerability again. But it was impossible to know when these incidents would occur.

During the process to receive psychotherapy with Maria, she asked me whether Ian ever drove his car erratically. At the time it felt like a really odd question, however, the answer was obviously a resounding 'yes'. I was advised that this was another characteristic of narcissistic abuse in that they often used their vehicle to manipulate control and fear.

Maria continued to explain that narcissists manipulate and exploit their victims' fears, including the fear of abandonment, so as to maintain control and power over them. The narcissist's need for validation, sees them use various tactics to ensure that their needs are met. Playing on the victim's fear of abandonment is one such method they may employ to ensure that the person remains tethered to them. Ian would have calculated early on in our relationship that I feared abandonment, which meant that he deliberately appeared to cater for my needs in offering commitment, which earned him my trust. Nonetheless, this then placed me on a rug that he could choose when to pull it from beneath my feet.

Maria stated that it is likely that he was also motivated by my negative memories of car trips with my mother. While it was impossible to say whether he knew that his dangerous driving often triggered my anxiety to the extent of wanting to jump from the moving vehicle; she said that stimulating my fear would have certainly given him great satisfaction.

Sadly, in my attempt to always appease him and to seek his approval and affection, I cannot rule out that I may have confessed the level of fear I experienced when he drove at high speeds; I never referred to his driving as dangerous to him direct as I would never choose to criticise anything he did. Nor can it be ruled out that he felt my anxiety and saw me sitting on my hands, thus, he was able to calculate the intention behind my action.

'Anyone can be manipulated by a narcissist. It has nothing to do with your level of intelligence, or how many degrees you have. Victims of narcissistic abuse often feel stupid for allowing themselves to be taken advantage of by narcissists. We are not taught to protect ourselves from these predators. We are also not taught the nature of who we are dealing with. Most of us didn't know people like this existed. We were completely unprepared to deal with this insidious manipulatory abuse'.

[Quote: Maria Consiglio]

6

Red Flags: Exploitation / Devaluation

One of the many narcissist red flags is their readiness to exploit others without guilt or remorse, all in the pursuit of meeting their own needs or personal gain. Narcissists view relationships as transactional rather than emotional connections. In the process of exploitation, the narcissist will show no regard or empathy for their victim's emotions or interests. This often occurs when the other person is in a subservient position, where it's awkward or impossible to resist the narcissist.

After the initial phase of idealisation, the narcissist will shift into the extremely painful devaluation stage, which is part of the narcissist abuse cycle: idealisation, devaluation, and discard. The, once adored partner now experiences the devaluation stage, where the narcissist starts to criticise, belittle, or demean them. This change can be sudden and bewildering, leaving the partner feeling emotionally wounded and confused. The narcissist may undermine their accomplishments, mock their interests, or make them question their worth.

This devaluation is often accompanied by a withdrawal of affection and intimacy, creating an atmosphere of emotional distance. It's during this phase that the true dynamics of the relationship become more apparent. This phase highlights the destructive patterns and the impact of the narcissist's behaviour on the partner's self-esteem and well-being.

Arguably, my entire relationship with Ian was exploitative from the very start: love-bombing, gaslighting and stonewalling are all forms of exploitation: the word is defined as 'the action or fact of treating someone unfairly in order to benefit from their work.' Therefore, there are many red flags that overlap in description and action.

Nonetheless, Ian was a master of exploitation in all areas of his life. He used people, even family and friends, to always benefit himself. Every meet-up or connection had an agenda, thus always *transactional rather than emotional;* which is a phrase that I believe accurately sums up how Ian viewed me. I was simply a commodity; someone to serve his needs and yet, the reality was that he was capable of exploiting my need to be loved by initially acting as some kind of knight in shining armour who wanted to rescue me.

When I think of exploitation and how that played out in my relationship with Ian, I feel that the biggest example of this relates to our sexual and intimate connection, which is an area that has caused the biggest confusion and the most emotional pain. The confusion stems from not realising that our sexual and intimate relationship was abusive. It pushes me into a zone of feeling that I've no right to complain or accuse, because the latter destroys lives if not true.

There are thousands of rape and sexual abuse cases and non-consensual sex incidents globally every single day: rape within relationships, workplace exploitation and lives ravaged by the misuse of the Internet and social media to non-consensual sexual exploitation. Therefore, if I didn't realise that I was being abused, how on earth can I sit alongside the thousands of others suffering from emotional and physical sexual trauma, claiming I understand? Was I not consenting to every single liaison, or had I simply shut down; gone into some kind of protective survival mode that normalised the coldness, the almost routine procedure of sexual contact?

The first time we had sex was at the hotel that had been intended as a wedding venue for my marriage to Hugh. It was the first time that I'd been intimate with anyone without really knowing what feelings I had for them. Afterwards, I felt empty, but had placed this mood on my lack of relationship experience and the fact that I was still grieving for Hugh. I believed that time would heal, and that the connection between Ian and I would grow; he too had experienced the loss of a loved one, Eva. So, I told myself that if he didn't want to be with me, that we simply would not be in a relationship.

However, his affection never transitioned from sex to love-making, it was only ever sex; it was functionary and therefore, always lacked emotional depth. As for physical contact, Ian disliked showing any 'affection' publicly, which meant that intimacy only ever occurred in the bedroom. Therefore, Ian was not prone to ever stealing kisses or cuddles from me; he never gabbed my hand to get me up to dance; I was never invited to curl up next to him on the sofa to watch a movie; instead, we sat separately. He never looked at me with eyes that spoke of admiration or love: I believed that only happened in romantic films or novels. I thought what I wanted was an impossible idealisation of what I thought love looked like; I believed that to be loved like a movie heroine that I needed to change everything about myself.

In the bedroom, although Ian knew that I'd been sexually abused in childhood and attacked as a teenager, he did nothing to make me feel safe. He never checked in with me to ask if I was okay, likewise, not once did he ensure that his actions felt right or good for me. He never told me that I was beautiful or sexy or desired; sex was just sex: devised to ensure that I always knew how lucky that someone like me, with my many flaws, was to have someone as amazing as him.

During an incident in my teenage years, I was attacked by a local man, who threatened to bite off my nipples if I didn't lie still. I fought like a wild cat to escape, and I did, but the repercussions of that event left me scarred for over thirty years. I was unable to have anyone touch my breasts; I hated it, and the very thought made me feel physically sick. Any move toward anyone touching my breasts would cause me to twist and turn to avoid contact. It also meant that as a mother, breastfeeding was not an option for me.

I do understand that not everyone knows how to deal with someone who has been through something of this nature. This is especially true when I reflect on my younger years, when I am now able to accept that Mac was not emotionally mature enough to deal with my stuff; after all, he was just 20-years-old when we got married; I was seventeen.

But Ian was a mature man when we met. He had an ex-wife, a late partner and had fathered two children, therefore, I didn't feel that it was unreasonable to believe that some of his experience could be more empathetic toward my own needs. Yet, Ian's method of dealing with my 'breast issues' was either to just not touch them at all; not coerce or coax me into a sense of feeling safe to be touched.

Instead, when I least expected it, he would periodically tweak my nipples, which I absolutely detested. It was always painful, physically, and emotionally. This small mindless act would churn painful unhealed memories and leave me wondering why, he would do something that he knew brought me great emotional discomfort. If I ever questioned him, he claimed that it had been done for fun; it was me who needed to lighten up.

Nonetheless, this created tension and fear during sex; the lack of empathy and consideration he showed toward my physical needs triggered feelings of being devalued. This pushed me into a negative emotional place whereby, I began to feel that sex was a duty, not something that was done for pleasure. Sex felt like his ownership.

I accept that in adulthood, we are responsible for dealing with our own emotional baggage; for seeking healing from unresolved issues. But real love, on a soul level, allows each person to unfold and peel back their many layers at a speed that is comfortable for them. It's about exploration and finding one another's boundaries, but I was unable to do that. I was so used to normalising *bad behaviour* and while technically our relationship was consensual, I was also normalising anything that made me feel uneasy because whenever I felt apprehensive, once again, I would prioritise people-pleasing over my own comfort levels.

For two decades, Ian and I slept in separate bedrooms. While many couples sleep separately for a number of reasons, Walt advised that in my case, that this was also a narcissistic trait. He advised that Ian's inability to connect emotionally and the fact that we only shared a bed during the love-bombing phase but slept separately from the moment I moved in with him, was a definite red flag.

Separate bedrooms allowed Ian to be in full control of all physical and sexual contact. This permitted him to dominate when sex occurred and by allowing me to sleep alone, it created further isolation. It also produced a certain level of anxiety because I would be permanently on standby for whenever Ian wanted sex; this meant that I could never fully relax. The uncertainty didn't create sexual expectancy or excitement, it instilled unease.

The expectant feeling reminded me of childhood. My mother used to drink; she mixed alcohol with medication for depression and this created severe violent mood swings. I would lie in bed listening for her footsteps on the stairwell; terrified that she would enter into my room looking for a fight. If dad was home, he got the brunt of it. However, if it was just my sister and I, it was potluck who she picked on.

Therefore, waiting for Ian to come into my bedroom at night, created that same sense of dread. He was never violent, but he was emotionally detached, and sex always had elements of what to me, felt degrading. Sleeping separate also meant that he didn't have to engage in post sex affection. His behaviour toward me made sex feel uneasy, and it was this unease that continued to contribute to the constant destruction of my confidence. Because I lacked confidence, it also meant that Ian would never be caught off guard by me unexpectedly wandering into his bedroom wanting sex, so he always knew his privacy wouldn't be disturbed.

Sex with Ian always followed the same pattern. It would include him telling me how good he was sexually, and how Eva had claimed that he was the best lover she'd ever had. Thus, sex was just another stunt for him to use to remind me of how lucky I was to have him; especially when, according to him, I was excessively flawed.

As early on as the first few weeks of relocating to live with Ian in Devon, there was a series of incidents that should have acted as warnings. But this was at a time, early 2000s, when the subject of narcissistic abuse wasn't readily discussed nor Internet information accessible at our fingertips.

As a result, after being offered the use of Eva's clothes, forbidden to hang pictures and photos on the walls, or to remove any of her possessions to place my own; it came as no surprise that Ian had also failed to remove her sex toys and naked photographs from the bedside drawers. He had allocated a drawer to me for my use, and yet, had left their intimate memories for me to find, which was hugely insensitive.

Another incident that springs to mind is Ian's claim, during sex, that he had the gift to hypnotise people. I've no idea, what prompted or where this claim originated, but he would go as far as attempting to put me into a hypnotic state. I was inexperienced both in relationships and sexually, which meant I had no idea what to expect in the bedroom. Nonetheless, Ian claiming that he could put me into a trance state definitely made me feel very uneasy.

I would feign feeling sleepy and close my eyes and listen to him talking. He told me that my name was Candy and that when I opened my eyes, I would become her. As Candy, I would listen and carry out his demands. This was way beyond my comfort zone, and so I would suddenly 'feign' waking up from a trance state and pretend that I couldn't remember what had just occurred. Where this would have led if I'd gone along with the game, I never found out; it scared me and thus, created another area of tension relating to sex and intimacy. Eventually, because I wasn't submissive to this game, it phased out after a few months.

Ian enjoyed what I can only refer to as a form of voyeurism. He was less inclined to have physical contact, preferring to observe. His other penchant was the use of sex toys, which while healthy and fun in many relationships, allowed the union to be more about gratification than contact. His job was basically done if I climaxed and vice-versa; it was often a little bit too rough and always performed with detachment.

Afterwards, he would praise himself on his ability to make a woman orgasm. Yet internally, I had just wanted it to be over, because after years of being compared to Eva, sex felt painfully humiliating. Reaching a climax gave him what he needed, the lengths I would go to please him was extraordinary. If I came, he associated that with giving me pleasure and was completely numb and blind to the depths of my true feelings, the deep rooted insecurity, lack of confidence and inferiority. Complexities all fuelled by him.

If the physical aspect of sex wasn't demeaning enough, it was the way he spoke to me during sex that really upset me. Whenever he talked dirty to me, he never spoke about what he would like to do to me; instead, he always spoke of a third person and what he would like to watch them do to me. I cannot bring myself to repeat what he said, my writing doesn't need to give his cruelness energy. But it was twisted, and I think even for the most sexually adventurous, there is a place within most of us that still needs to feel safe and loved because intimacy opens up vulnerabilities.

What makes it more difficult to comprehend is that Ian knew that I'd been sexually assaulted and abused during childhood years; therefore, it was difficult to get my head around why he would want to imagine and explicitly talk about someone else having sex with me. It felt offensive and degrading. I would hold back tears and later when I was alone again, I would cry myself to sleep. And yet, still I stayed. My belief that I couldn't survive without him felt real. I convinced myself that this was the very definition of love even though every part of my mind, body and soul was deeply unhappy.

I continued to write including adaptations of Ian's story, which because he never read any of my work, allowed me the freedom to edit his recordings, to create a heroic protagonist that was more likeable; I guess I was crafting a more affable version of him.

One day while he was away in London, I decided that I should consider backing my work up on a USB stick: it was something that Ian had instilled in me. There was an area of his desk that stored stationery items which I was free to use. I borrowed a USB stick from his desk and inserted it into my computer. The screen of my PC came up with a message stating that there was an error on the memory stick. The message enquired whether I wanted the error to be fixed and I selected 'OK'. Within minutes hundreds of pornographic images were restored onto the memory stick.

I realise that a mass majority of people view and enjoy porn. But what was really unsettling about the images I discovered, is that in what was well over 200 photographs, every single image was of a female teenager. A majority of the images had a copyright mark in the corner and the marking suggested that the site was dedicated purely to images of teen girls.

Some of the girls didn't look old enough to be on the site; some didn't look much older than my daughter. They were all younger than Ian's daughter, and possibly young enough to be his granddaughter. Out of all the unease I'd felt with Ian, I'd never imagined him to be the kind of man who would gain pleasure from looking at images of young girls.

If the images had been of adults, I would have still been disappointed, but at least, it would, in my opinion, have felt more acceptable; something that I could pass off as a natural curiosity. But teen girls, some of them appearing to be very young, felt deeply and worryingly exploitative. I wondered whether he ever thought of my daughter in this way; I also questioned how he would feel if men viewed similar images of her; I needed to know what his boundaries were as a stepfather figure.

More disturbing, if it could get any worse, was that every single teen girl, hundreds of them, was sat in exactly the same position. Each had a sex toy inserted into their vagina.

Also restored to the USB file was three separate folders; these were labelled, Eva, Noelia, and Chloe. Inside each of these folders were more pornographic images. What was notable about these files and the images stored within each, is the very distinct characteristics of the women. None of the images were clearly of the three of us, but what I believed, were Ian's mental depiction of us. I know nothing about pornography or art, but the images of Eva and Noelia were very 'classy'; black and white photographs of incredibly beautiful women, whose images weren't sexually graphic, but what I would describe as more artfully seductive.

However, in the file labelled Chloe, the images were in colour and the women were what you could say, 'less attractive'; they were all also women of a larger size. The images were very sexually graphic; less arty and what felt more sluttish. I didn't feel that I needed a degree in psychology to understand Ian's inner and deeper thoughts toward me when creating these files.

The bottom fell out of my world.

I had no idea what to do or how concerned I should be; I was in shock. I knew that looking at the imagines didn't mean that he necessarily would view Lauren or her friends in that way; but the focus on that age group did disturb me. It was still at a time when this kind of material wasn't readily available on the Internet, therefore, it felt like Ian had done a lot of work, spent tons of hours in researching to create the files. Likewise, discussing feelings regarding the viewing of pornography, either personally or relating to partners, wasn't something that my friends and I ever discussed. I'm not saying that it was a taboo subject, it just wasn't on my radar. I had no idea whether this was a deal breaker or not.

So, for the first time, I called Walt. Prior to working in the DVU (Domestic Violence Unit), he had worked in a unit dealing with crimes relating to indecent images of children. He had a daughter of his own and knew better than most, the mindset relating to this subject. I wanted to know, first and foremost, whether I should be concerned regarding Lauren and also, if Ian had acted illegally; if so, I wanted advice on what to do.

Walt advised me that Ian's actions were far too common and sadly, not illegal, because the images had been sourced on a mainstream website, which suggested that the girls' images were consensual. Likewise, because the images were watermarked with the site address, even if the girls appeared young, the nature of delivery of the material suggested that the girls were of legal age.

Walt advised that Ian's actions was not a precursor for him to act inappropriately with Lauren, but he could understand my concerns. He said that most often, people who viewed indecent images, were able to separate their fantasy from real life. What disturbed him as a police officer, was the fact that most pornographic images of young people, were in fact stolen; at the time, somewhere in the region of 80%+.

This meant that a scenario such as a teen girl sending a naked photo of herself to a boyfriend or to someone she liked, could get into the wrong hands, and be used illegally. Therefore, when someone like Ian specifically seeks out this age group, over 80% of the girls were likely to have not given their consent to the image being used. This data was relevant at the time; I can only hope things have changed. Nonetheless, this advice came some 12 years before I would call Walt for more relationship advice.

On this occasion, I had no choice but to tackle Ian because I couldn't ignore my anger, fear, hurt or disgust at his behaviour. I also thought that he needed to know that not only could the images have been stolen and potentially be of underage girls. I wanted him to really think about the impact of this on us as a family. Additionally, if I could accidentally find this 'secret' out about him, what would happen if someone else discovered that he liked to look at indecent images of teen girls: Lauren, his daughter, friends, or business acquaintances? I wanted to ask him as a father, whether he truly felt that it was appropriate and whether his male friends, if they knew, would think it acceptable when they too had daughters of their own.

I wasn't judging his desire or need to look at pornographic images, I felt that I wasn't in a position to dictate that to him. But I did feel that I had a right to express that the age group and legality of some of the images was definitely questionable and didn't portray him in a way that was admirable. For someone who needed to be admired, this wasn't how Ian wanted anyone, including myself, to see him.

I vented my anger and disappointment at him; this was the first and only time I ever spoke to Ian with unfiltered words. He did apologise and in hindsight, perhaps an apology was a small price for him to pay to ensure that he didn't lose overall control within our relationship.

I didn't tell Ian that I had spoken to Walt about him. But I did tell him that in previous conversations with Walt as a friend, that I knew that a large proportion of images were illegal and emphasised to Ian that he may have been looking at stolen photographs of vulnerable, underage, girls. Ian knew that my friendship with Walt was as a result of a previous professional connection and that our association had continued because my friend would often give me advice relating to any police content in my scriptwriting work.

It was a relationship that didn't threaten Ian, due to distance and an age difference. Thus, I would often tell him about Walt's script feedback and other professional, work related stories. Therefore, it didn't come as a surprise to Ian, that I would have data relating to teen pornography, either gained from work related conversation with Walt or his subsequent supervision to advise on the darker material my husband had encouraged me to write.

I spoke to Ian of my disgust and the kind of people Walt had to deal with as a police officer working to protect young girls. It was the first time I'd seen Ian appear vulnerable, if not, almost fearful. Perhaps it was the exposure of his not so perfect side that made him seem this way.

With my anger boiling over, I also addressed the topic of the three folders and told Ian how offensive I had found the content. I told him that I had found it disturbing that he would use the memory of Eva in such a shocking way. I asked him to think about what Eva would think about his actions and especially, him also portraying her best friend, Noelia, in that way too. I then spoke of the hurt he had caused me in portraying me in such a negatively comparative way to versions of Eva and Noelia. I wanted him to explain to me why he had created the folders using our three names.

Ian's explanation was almost worse than the action itself. He told me that for 'amusement' he had gone online pretending to be one of the women; Eva, Noelia, or Chloe, and that under those names and images, he had flirted with men under the pretence of being them. He claimed that he had been fascinated by the responses to the images, which had included, also pretending to be one of the teen girls.

I asked him, why he had constructed such a contrast between 'myself' and the images of Eva and Noelia. Bluntly, he told me that they both represented the 'perfect woman,' whereas, I didn't.

I've no idea, how mentally or emotionally, I ever made a comeback from this episode of my life. Perhaps I never did, not until I removed myself from the situation. But there are no words to explain the pain that his explanation caused. I knew that I was far from perfect, but to be told that I, in his eyes, would never live up to what he looked for in a woman, killed me on the inside.

His comment literally destroyed the last bit of self-respect or self-love, I had for myself. It plunged me into the deepest level of unworthiness that made me feel hideous to even look at. To top this, his explanation for his online charade, pretending to be one of us, seemed unbelievable. He had spoken as if his *alleged honesty* was something to be admired, seemingly completely oblivious to how 'sick' he sounded, admitting that he had paraded under our names, including his late, dead, partner. Therefore, if he was lying, I dreaded to think what the truth was going to be. I had no idea how I was supposed to come to terms being with a man who had just admitted that he was deviant enough to engage online in this way; this felt almost worse than simply looking at pornography, teen girls aside. Nonetheless, the incident crushed me completely. I wish I'd had my wits about me and had left at that moment. But I stayed.

What is even worse, Lauren was in her bedroom when I had the initial argument with Ian regarding the images; she heard every word. I told Ian that Lauren had overheard the nature of our discussion. I did this to safeguard any complications further down the Lne; I didn't want there to be any incident whereby it appeared that I'd voluntarily shared the discovery with my daughter, who was old enough to understand the content and subsequently my upset.

However, I don't think that it proved to be a good idea to tell Ian that Lauren had overheard our argument, because I think that this made him feel vulnerable; as the narcissist he would have really disliked anything that challenged his perfect self-image. Thus, while I can't say that Lauren and Ian's relationship was perfect, she certainly respected him, and did love him as a father figure. Therefore, for Lauren to have any negative viewpoint of Ian, would have meant that he had lost his natural control, one that comes from the entitlement of parenthood, over Lauren.

As a result, Ian became a much harder taskmaster as a father figure, which resulted in me failing her yet again, when he basically threw her out of our home without warning; she was 18-years old. Out of fear, I did nothing to challenge or to stop him. For days, I begged him to re-think regarding his actions, but he made me choose between him and my daughter. I'd been with him for years and I was too deeply entrenched in the belief that I could not survive without him.

Lauren's crime was to hang out with some unfavourable guys, to consistently return home later than agreed and to fail to do her schoolwork. The usual teen stuff. It was an awful period of my life, and one that, in the hindsight of wisdom, as the woman I am now becoming, I would certainly handle very differently.

As the years passed, it took Lauren quite some time to forgive me for not having her back. I think it affected her a great deal because in essence, she was discarded when she became too troublesome. Agreeably, she was very taxing, but her behaviour was relatively mild in comparison to what she could have been. However, I did what I could and was able to persuade Ian to allow us to give Lauren money to pay for rent and food each month, until she was fully able to stand on her own two feet.

Ian's remorse regarding the discovery of the images was very short-lived. I felt extremely low after this incident, which had in my mind, also contributed toward Lauren no longer liver at home, which resulted in me becoming very distant. I think this prompted Ian to react threateningly so that he could regain control, because while I was withdrawn and could reasonably excuse myself for not being the all-singing, all-dancing wife that he expected me to be, I think he didn't know how to deal with me in a state that suggested that my behaviour could potentially be totally erratic and unpredictable.

I knew better than to repeat my angst to Ian over and over again, but I did tell him that I needed time to think things over and this was my way of explaining my own silence and distant mood. But I hadn't realised until now, that requesting time to mull things over, would have placed him in a position of uncertainty and he wouldn't have liked that at all.

His response to my need for space, within a week, was to tell me that he wasn't going to allow me to bang him on the head time and time again; an accusation similar to the one he had made when I had asked, just once, whether he loved me. It felt as though he knew that if he portrayed me as some kind of 'nagging wife', that I would get upset and become vulnerable to rejection. He knew that I really disliked the derogatory, 'her indoors, ball and chain' references, because I felt that they really devalued the role of romantic partner or wife.

Thus, as far as Ian was concerned, he had apologised once and that was it as far as he was concerned. I was advised to basically shut up and put up, or to get out. Once more, he played on my fear of abandonment and my belief that I no longer had the ability to survive on my own. He literally banned me from ever speaking about my feelings or the incident itself. This meant, that in a split second, I had to choose to accept what he had done, or to leave.

So, once again, regardless of how it made me feel, I decided to stay, while at the same time being aware that because I had crossed him, I was fearful of the repercussions of doing so. I had to quickly but falsely pretend that I was capable of forgiving and forgetting the hundreds of teen girl images and the painful obvious comparison he had made between Eva, Noelia, and myself.

It was a case of my 'Services' were to be restored from immediate effect or else! I tried to continue as if nothing had happened, but each time he came into my bedroom, expecting me to perform my functionary sexual duties, it sickened me to the pit of my stomach. I think inside, I died a little bit more each time. I had surrendered and given him full control over me; switching off was the only way I could mentally survive.

Some months later, we went on an overseas business trip to visit Paul and Iris, which was during the four year success period of their venture. Ian booked us separate bedrooms at a beautiful 5-star hotel. The hotel was frequented by a lot of wealthy international local businessmen, and I state men, because I'm referring to witnessing a culture whereby men were still in the main, those in this position.

I spent a lot of time on my own, while Ian visited his brother at their office. I had conversations with owners of small shops and restaurants, who had witnessed their businesses decline in favour of the introduction of the large hotels and an influx of rich people moving to the tax haven the country offered; the same people who preferred 5-star luxury.

It was during these conversations I witnessed a very beautiful Russian woman speaking in English to a male stranger. She told him that she wanted to go to his hotel room for sex. She told the man that her husband had a different mistress every weekend and that she lived local, where she spent most of her time alone, while her husband did what he wanted. She admitted to being lonely and stated that she was sure that even if she died, her husband wouldn't notice. The conversation made me sad. I worried about her safety. Her story also prompted me to reflect on my own situation.

Back at the hotel, I began to notice that a lot of the men were accompanied by very young girls; who without prejudice, their behaviour suggested that they weren't daughters of the men. This too saddened me; were they happy and if not, I wondered if they would end up like me. Trapped and unable to run.

Nonetheless, it made me think of Ian's penchant for teen girls and his outrageously bizarre explanation for his actions. I felt like a caged animal, not able to be free to speak my mind. I felt used and humiliated and tired of keeping my hurt under wraps.

One breakfast, I mentioned the conversation I'd overheard between the Russian woman and the male stranger. I went on to talk about the men I'd seen in the elevator with their young female companions. I used the third party mind game against Ian, knowing full well that my mention of the disgust I felt against 'these men', that he would see right through me. At first, he was very calm and spoke of needing to get to the office and suggested that I may like to go with him. I was surprised by his seeming lack of reaction, but it came later, when I was in the car.

He drove for a little while and then he stopped on the side of the road in blazing hot sunshine and shouted at me to get out of the car. He told me that he'd had enough of my whining. When I refused to get out, he got out of the driver side and walked around to my door and opened it. At first, he didn't touch me, but kept on telling me to get out; I think he was mindful that other drivers were witnessing this exchange. However, as soon as the coast was clear, he managed to pull me out of the car, crying and begging, for him to not do this to me.

As I watched him drive off, I mentally went into meltdown as panic began to set in. The level of fear I experienced was the worse I'd felt since Hugh's death. My bag was in the boot of the car, so I had no money, no passport or water. I was stranded on the roadside; the anxiety made my breathing laboured, my chest was pounding, and I also felt this odd sense of pins and needles all over my body. My vision began to blur, and I could hardly focus.

I considered what would happen if I fainted on the roadside. I started to sing *ten green bottles* in my head and attempted to distract myself with thoughts of whether hitchhiking back to the hotel was a safe option; I decided not. I considered what would happen if I just started to walk and walk; would I walk to happiness and freedom, or would it end in total tragedy. I opted to start walking in the direction of the hotel; I had no idea how far it was.

I then began to blame myself for what was happening to me; if I'd just kept my mouth shut none of this would have happened. I walked for about 20 minutes and then I saw Ian on the opposite side of the road. He had pulled over into a layby and was waiting. I wasn't sure if he expected me to run, to not keep him waiting, but a part of me didn't want to look too desperate. I was also fearful that he would drive off just as I reached the car, and I didn't want him to see how much I was shaking; almost shivering as if cold on a scorching hot day.

Ian didn't drive off. I was allowed back into the car and for the remainder of the trip he told me how things were going to be for the rest of our married life. That I wouldn't question him or humiliate him. That I wouldn't keep banging him on the head for something he did that had been and gone, buried in the past. If I wasn't in agreement with this arrangement then he was more than happy for me to go and find my own Mr Perfect, because frankly, according to him, they didn't exist.

He then listed all of my flaws and reminded me that no one would want me; that I was lucky to have him and lucky to have the life he offered me. I was scared, this really felt like this was the last straw, and that I had to do anything to win him back; to show him how much I appreciated him. I spent the rest of the journey trying to appease him and promising to do whatever I needed to do to make him happy again; the cost was rough sex that allowed him to basically do what he wanted with me.

This was to be the beginning of the kind of sex we would have for the rest of his active sexual years. His preference was for me to 're-enact' the images he had preferred with the teen girls. Every time, it would always be the same routine; sex toys, no contact between us and him telling me what he would like to see other men do to me. He used degrading language that got repeatedly worse over time. I cannot repeat what he said, because it physically repulses me. I cannot put the energy of his words into the beautiful world I am still creating for myself. Nonetheless, I lived for years performing whatever degrading sex Ian required, while I continued to be completely starved of any true affection, love, or gentle intimacy. This was the price I paid to not be abandoned.

Toward the final years of our relationship, Ian began to have problems getting an erection. His testosterone levels became very low, and he sought medical advice. He was given medication and a gel, but it didn't work. When we moved to Spain, he tried a different medical route, and the doctors were very obliging; they could see that I was a much younger woman to him, and they wanted to help us have a 'normal and healthy sex life.'

Inside my head, I felt guilty for begging my Holy Father to never allow Ian to have sex with me again; I was secretly praying that the medication wouldn't work. This occurred at the same time as the regular synchronicities and angelic numbers and formed part of my long overdue realisation that my relationship with Ian was far from healthy or normal.

Thus, I hadn't been aware until it was highlighted in part by Walt and further explored by Maria, that I'd been a victim of sexual abuse. At the time of Manuel Angel's question as to whether I'd ever been sexually abused, I was surprised that he was able to detect trauma that had occurred in my childhood years. However, it had been the present abuse this beautiful soul was detecting.

Thankfully, my pray to never have sex with Ian again, was answered.

'Love doesn't die a natural death.
Love has to be killed, either by neglect or narcissism.'

[Source: lovesagame.com]

7

Red Flags: Jealousy / Possessiveness

Narcissists often grapple with feelings of envy. These sentiments can spark a range of behaviours, from controlling tendencies to resentment. The common theme is the narcissist's need to protect their fragile ego, which results in them projecting their own feelings of envy onto others and tearing others down to maintain their own sense of superiority.

Likewise, possessiveness is another red flag relating to a narcissist in a romantic relationship. While it may feel flattering at first, it isn't a healthy attribute. Narcissists may display controlling behaviours fuelled by jealousy, seeking to restrict their partner's interactions and activities. They might become overly suspicious, questioning their partner's loyalty, and interpreting innocent situations as threats to their control. Possessiveness stems from their deep-seated insecurities and the desire to maintain a tight grip on their partner's life.

Until I started to attend my sessions with the psychotherapist, Maria, in Spain, it had never even occurred to me that Ian was capable of feeling jealousy toward me. I'd spent twenty years trying to please him, attempting to live up to the high standards he had set; the goal always to become more like Eva. Perhaps throwing Noelia into the mix should have given me a deeper insight into Ian's truest desires; maybe Noelia was the preferred French woman out of the two, but Ian knew that she was already taken and so settled for Eva. Conceivably, Eva may have known this, but her life was too short to allow it to take emotional priority. Nonetheless, while I don't really need to know the answer to this interrogation, what remains is the fact that I spent two decades attempting to fill one or both of their shoes.

As a result, I was in a vicious cycle of unachievable self-improvement unaware of the reality that it served Ian's agenda for me to not be like them. Reaching perfection and finding confidence in myself didn't serve his need to maintain control over me. However, because of the extreme low self-esteem I experienced it never struck me that Ian could still have envious feelings in relation toward me in any respect. While I can recognise that any form of success can stir the green-eyed monster in a relationship, even in the healthiest partnerships, I had always considered in a 'romantic' relationship that envy was linked to concerns regarding fidelity. In this respect, I was convinced that I was unattractive, undesirable, and unlovable, that no one, other than Ian, would ever want to be with me. Because of this deep-rooted belief, it was therefore, unimaginable to contemplate that Ian could ever feel jealous of me.

However, according to Maria, jealousy is one of the main driving points of a narcissist to destroy their victim. She explained that the narcissist sees in their victim attributes that they aren't capable of; this is the root of their jealousy. In my case, she said that it could have been qualities such as gentleness, empathy, and likeability; it was true, Ian didn't possess any of these virtues. She also used the word beauty, which made me derisively scoff,

"I'm not beautiful."

My comment was duly noted.

Therefore, as Maria continued to explain, in a narcissistic relationship, the narcissist will be driven by resentment to take possession of their victim. Often, they will cleverly mirror their target, copy their qualities, to lure them into a false sense of oneness: in a romantic context, finding their perfect match. Thus, feeling a strong connection, the victim fully opens up, which enables the narcissist to learn everything they need to know about them, including discovering their weak points, which are then ultimately used against their prey to destroy them. The goal is to manipulate the victim to attain full control.

Thus, Ian's need to belittle and quash my positive qualities was driven by jealousy in a need to protect his fragile ego, while fuelling his own sense of superiority. And while he never expressed his jealousy by questioning my romantic loyalty to him, any interest or regret I ever showed regarding my career, or desire to live my life in a different way, thus suggesting that something was more important to me than him, was viewed as being disloyal and therefore, something that he needed to manage to maintain full control.

I was faithful to Ian for the entirety of our relationship. Because of past abuse, I never looked at another man in a sexual way, that just isn't me. Of course, I can recognise and appreciate when someone is attractive, but that applies to all people; for me stating that someone is good-looking or pretty, is factual, but it doesn't mean that I'm mentally undressing them.

In the two decades I was with Ian, I had one serious crush on a fitness instructor at my local gym. I was very fond of the guy, Wills, because for a period of time, we trained together, and he helped me to believe in myself and to transform me from couch-potato into a gym junkie. He also helped me to believe that I was capable of anything and that I could take back control of my weight, which ultimately helped me to have a more positive body image.

I think Wills filled a void that I didn't at the time realise needed filling; he spoke to me encouragingly and positively. He made me feel seen and heard. He made me feel good about myself and I liked the attention. As a result, I found myself looking forward to seeing him.

However, my thoughts were very grounded, I could see the relationship for what it was. Wills was a paid gym instructor; it was his job to make his clients feel good about themselves. Therefore, I didn't doubt that other clients had the same experience of him, because he was really good at his job. Nonetheless, there was a part of me that really wanted to fancy him in a more sexual manner, but I simply couldn't see him in that way. Not only did it feel disloyal to Ian to think of Wills sexually, but I was also aware that sex didn't interest me; I craved something much more meaningful.

In the heart of me, what I actually needed, was the kind of love and intimacy that comes from a profoundly spiritual connection. Needless, to say, Wills was more of an innocent schoolgirl crush, the kind that put butterflies in my tummy and made my cheeks flush whenever he said hello to me. But I liked it that way, because it was my first notable experience of beginning to feel good about myself: almost an awakening, albeit late in life, to my own womanhood. I can see how sexual abuse, visible and invisible forms, can stunt this growth.

There is just the one occasion that I recall Ian expressing some jealousy, which occurred around about the same time I was working out at the gym with Wills. We were living at the Hampshire rental property and the landlord sent a couple of handymen round to finish off some work on the fixtures and fittings; the property was a new build. One of the workmen noticed my blonde curly hair and commented that my hair was similar to his own; he had it tied back for work purposes. His colleague had found this amusing, which triggered some playful banter and the guy letting down his hair to show me. Their work took them a few days to complete, so the laughter continued over several breaktime mugs of tea and biscuits. I got to know their names and the only reason I remember the name of the guy with the curly hair, is because Ian and I, had a friend with the same name, Nigel.

As mentioned, I found Ian's penchant for talking explicitly about other men having sex with me degrading, and while it probably was a turn-on for him, I found it upsetting. I did attempt to discuss my feelings with Ian, but I was told that it was just a bit of fun and that he found the idea of other men being attracted to me sexy. I stopped trying to talk to him about my feelings and instead, tried to tell myself that it was harmless. I attempted to find comfort in the fact that the men in question were fictitious, they had no name; the talk was about the action of the men and what they did to me and not about the men themselves.

One night, Nigel's name unexpectedly popped up during the usual sex routine. The name caught me off guard because my instinct was to think about our friend of the same name and not some workman who I had only just met. I found Ian's sexual language generally repulsive, but the mention of a friend's name during sex left me feeling more affronted than normal. I found it impossible to hide my feelings, so I had to say something. I told him that using a friend's name during 'sexual play' made me feel very uncomfortable, to which it then became apparent that Ian was referring to the workman.

As soon as I realised that Ian was talking about the other Nigel, I recognised that this was the first and only time I ever saw a jealous and more vulnerable side to my husband; but I was also aware that he was testing me. For some couples, this kind of sexual role play may be viewed as harmless fun; but for me, all I could think of was that if Ian really knew me, he would know that I found his comments distressing; adding a name of a known person added humiliation.

I told Ian that the use of a known person's name was a total turn-off for me and returned to my bedroom. In this scenario, I felt that the odds were stacked against me. I could have gone unwillingly along with Ian's game just to please him sexually, but the fear of believing I found another man attractive was not a risk worth taking, because I sensed that it would be used against me at some point. Therefore, the safer option was to leave and to express my disgust, which also allowed me to escape another session of unpleasant sex. I was always in survival mode. In my room, I cried as if I didn't want to see another day; even then, I felt that it was my own sexual inadequacy that had created this mind fuck.

Another form of jealousy I was informed, was Ian's need to say derogatory things about anyone associated with my past or any of my previous successes such as my career or simple personal attributes. He condemned everything that was part of my life because he wanted me to see him as providing me with everything I could possibly need or want. He spoke badly about my Yorkshire home, media career, friends, family, spiritual beliefs, accent, education (lack of), and of Hugh and Mac, which I did pull him up on.

He acted a little differently when it came to Lauren; if he ever said anything negative about her, it could easily be taken as parental concern or constructive criticism. He seemed to have a genuine soft spot for her and yet, he was also guilty of referring to her as 'your daughter', as in mine, whenever she did anything bad, but would act proud when she excelled; which is not unusual in self-made second families.

However, when it came to Ian's ability to create jealousy, he was a true master. I not only had years of being compared to Eva and Noelia, plus suffering the third party referral mind games; but he would openly express his attraction to another woman by simply staring at her. In the earlier part of our relationship, I would comment on his actions, to which he would offer one of two responses. If the woman in question was classically attractive, he would simply agree that he found her beautiful; he would then reel off a list of her fine attributes. If the woman in question was let's say, still attractive, but more sensually dressed, he would tell me that he wasn't a monk, meaning that he found her highly fuckable.

I realise that this isn't unique behaviour to someone with narcissistic traits, and that I'm not the first or the last person to witness their partner ogling someone else. I also realise that I'm responsible for loving myself first and foremost, and not depending on someone else for validation of my worth. But this behaviour was far from healthy, and it becomes unhealthy when someone deliberately acts in a way knowing that it devalues another person, especially someone they are supposed to love.

For Ian, this was just another way of extending the comparisons to Eva and Noelia, and the added pain was that he was asking me to almost visualise the kind of woman he would like to have sex with, which were females who were very different to myself. This was also a man who didn't touch me directly during sex; therefore, I was starved of affection and intimacy and yet, had to listen to him admitting that he found someone else intimately irresistible.

If I ever expressed how uncomfortable or upsetting, I found Ian's behaviour, I would be told that I was too sensitive or jealous. If I tried asking Ian to imagine how it would make him feel if I behaved toward him in the same way, he would tell me that it wouldn't matter to him, because he knew that he was handsome and that women looked at him all of the time. Hence, he was skilled at justifying his actions and twisting everything around so that I always appeared to be abnormally insecure.

To live in a constant form of survival mode is draining. I wasn't fighting for food or water, but internally I was wrestling to feel safe and wanted; I believed that Ian was my provider and protector and that without him I couldn't survive. Because of this, I warped my own boundaries and allowed myself to feel unease and to experience lack of self-respect in the deep belief that I was the actual problem; I needed to be more open-minded, confident, easy-going, fun, free, attractive, successful: the list was endless. If I was a stick of rock, the word running through my centre would be people-pleaser; I was programmed to place myself last.

During Ian's more affluent days, during the same period that I was training with Wills, he decided that we needed a housekeeper. Ginny seemed nice and the perfect fit for the job. She had recently been through a volatile divorce and was determined to get back on her own feet. She was doing several cleaning jobs, which suggested that she was hard working and responsible. She was also my age, so while Ian had previously suggested that I wasn't to make friends with the staff, referring to the former cleaner, Vicky; I saw in Ginny someone who would perhaps be a woman's woman and be of private support if needed. However, I couldn't have been more wrong about a person as I was with Ginny. She was hard working, literally buzzed with energy and was also always bright and bubbly. Likewise, she was also very attractive, and I quickly learnt that she knew exactly how to use this to her advantage; perhaps her own survival mechanism.

As a result, she quickly ingratiated herself into our lives to the point that she became Ian's main subject of conversation. He became concerned about her well-being, and offered her more hours because after-all, as he put it, I wasn't capable of keeping on top of the housework; I looked after the house well and even tidied the house before Ginny arrived. When I highlighted that I thought I did a good job, he twisted the suggestion into it being for my benefit, so that I could enjoy doing more of what I liked. He presented her as a type of useful gift to me; the person who could do all the jobs I disliked such as ironing and changing the beds.

I really didn't have a problem in employing someone to help them financially, and if affordable, I was happy to be alleviated from some of my household responsibilities. However, it was the way in which Ian proposed that Ginny should be given more hours. It felt that he was once again, weaponising another woman to instil inferiority in me.

It also soon became very clear that Ginny was having private conversations with Ian; I would walk into a room and catch her talking to him, but she would start cleaning as soon as she saw me. Shortly afterwards, she would single me out, and acting like some kind of best friend, would offer to make me a cup of coffee, while seemingly wanting to chat about my plans for the week.

Yet, later the same day, after Ginny had left; Ian would have some story about her plight, which he needed to help fix. Hence, the 'private conversations' would lead him to offering her more hours of work, a pay increase to reflect the responsibilities of her role, even though these didn't change, he also decided to give her a car so that she had a reliable mode of transport. Yet, the car given to her was a car 'gifted' to me by Ian.

I use the term 'gifted' somewhat loosely: Ian was also good at making it appear that he was extremely generous toward me, which yes, to a certain point that is true. But what he also did was make everything appear as though it was his decision to permit me to have something; everything was given in a form of unspoken reward system. Therefore, if you are in a partnership, in my case, one that was via marriage, and I also contributed financially and with other support as required; my input never earned me the position to call our alliance an equal 'us', it was always him seemingly providing for me, which gave him the self-appointed power to make all decisions.

Therefore, in this reward system the car given to Ginny was one that he 'gifted' to me, but because I didn't drive due to anxiety, he could justify giving it to someone else and use the excuse of my anxiety against me; likewise, in doing so, he could then also portray yet another female figure has having qualities I didn't possess, while at the same time boost his own ego because of the appreciation he earned from his generosity.

But it didn't stop at just the car. Ginny would house sit when we went away, which was useful, although the house had a live-linked security system. I would return home to find her bed unmade and the bathroom left uncleaned. I discovered her knickers in the unmade bed alongside one of my husband's shirts. The landlord provided a gardener who would gleefully report to Ian that Ginny had been sunbathing topless; they would then disappear to whisper like two schoolboys.

Ginny went from wearing jeans and a t-shirt for work to hot pants and a cropped top. I said nothing, because I was acknowledging that any jealousy I had toward her was my doing and something I needed to work on. I was still training with Wills, and I was changing shape, so there was an element of growing confidence; but as soon as this began to emerge, Ginny started to say things that were offensive to me.

I would return from the gym, and she would ask how I was doing with my weight loss regime; when I reported back my success, she would make a snide comment about me not looking any different. She would then start to talk about herself and claim that she couldn't understand why someone as attractive as her, didn't have a husband, when 'fat women' did. I was used to Ian's third person mind games, so I assumed she was referring to me as a 'fat wife.' Yet, regardless of how hurtful the comment felt, I couldn't be certain that it was directed at me. Life with Ian had pushed me to the point of not recognising natural boundaries, which meant that I always viewed other people's negative behaviour toward me as somehow my fault.

During this lavish period of our marriage, Ian decided to treat family and friends to a week away at a beautiful beach house in Devon to see in the New Year. The house had 8 bedrooms, which meant that because Ian and I had separate rooms, we could invite six couples to join us. Our first choice was naturally our children, Lauren, Ollie and Olivia, and their respective partners; but out of the three, only one could make it. We invited Ian's mum, Beryl, but she declined: she was at an age that she felt too old to be uprooted from her home. So, we invited friends and again, closer to the time, one couple dropped out. So, Ian took it upon himself to invite Ginny.

She accepted the invite and from there on her behaviour and sense of entitlement just went from bad to worse. Ginny claimed that she didn't have anything to take to wear for the get together, so Ian took it upon himself to give her a selection of Eva's clothing; after all, I didn't wear them, implying that they didn't fit me but would fit her perfectly.

I was then dragged around several shops when Ian took Ginny shopping for clothes; I stood by as she skipped out of the dressing room to show off a little black dress that my husband was buying for her. I even joined in to say how good she looked in the dress, because truth be known, she did look nice in the dress.

When it came to the New Year Devon break, Ginny was taken on a tour across Dartmoor and treated to lunch at a 5-star hotel. She was treated like part of our family and there genuinely was a part of me that felt okay with that; I wanted to be the kind of person who could do that for someone else, especially when they were trying to rebuild their life

On New Year's Eve there was 12 of us in total and we had an amazing three course dinner. I wasn't responsible for all of the food, some of it was contributed by family and friends; nonetheless, there was a lot of food and drink. Everyone ate a lot and drank a lot, and we had a lot of fun and laughter. We had a break between courses, and I went to organise dessert. I placed a choice of 4 puddings out for people to choose what they wanted and at that point Ginny looked at the desserts and piped up,

"I think Chloe is trying to make us as fat as her."

I don't think everyone heard the comment, but the people standing closest to her looked a bit taken aback; but then because I was too shocked to say anything, they seemed to brush it off as if they had misheard what had been said. Feeling suddenly stone cold sober, I also continued to hear the rest of what she had to say when talking to my friend's boyfriend, Charlie, about how she found it astounding that she couldn't get a decent man in her life when fat women could.

She then went on to tell Charlie how her ex had spray painted her car with the words 'gold-digger' and how much this had really upset her. Suddenly, it felt as though a lightbulb had been switched on in my head. Instead of viewing her with yes, jealousy, but also compassion and the wish to help her to start out again, I realised that her own survival mechanism was ruthless. It had taken a lot to get me to that point, but I recognised that I needed to be less trusting of her. Sadly, I knew that there was no point in telling Ian what I felt, as he would view my concerns as deep envy. Notably, it was Charlie that Ginny stayed up talking to until the early hours of the morning; I don't think my friend was impressed.

The predicament for me during all of the Ginny escapade, was that I truly had no sense of what was normal and acceptable behaviour. My need to always placate and to place other people's needs above my own, meant that my boundaries were severely warped.

When I told a few of my closest female friends in later years the Ginny story, they had some very choice words they would have said if placed in that situation; except, we all knew that they wouldn't have been put in that situation in the first place: and that's the part that really stings! I was used to being mistreated and devalued; this was my survival technique.

Therefore, by speaking to my friends, they helped me to realise that I needed them to say that it was okay, to give me permission, as an adult, to say if or when something isn't agreeable with me and to know that it is normal to set personal boundaries. They also reminded me that I'm a bright, professional, and sensitive woman, and that it is my time to shine. Their guidance and words helped me a lot. But what is harder to forget, what remains inside, is the knowing that my inner child never learnt how to say, no; and this has been exploited by Ian to its fullest.

'The narcissist relies on jealousy as a powerful emotion that can cause you to compete for his or her affections, so provocative statements like "I wish you'd be more like her," or "he wants me back into his life, I don't know what to do," are designed to trigger the abuse victim into competing and feeling insecure about his or her position in the narcissist's life.'

[Quote: Shahiba Arabi]

8

Red Flags: Lack of Accountability / Quick to Anger

Refusing to take responsibility for their actions or mistakes is a huge one on the narcissist red flag checklist. Narcissists are prone to shift blame onto others in order to maintain their inflated self-image. This lack of accountability provides a convenient escape from confronting their shortcomings and enables the perpetuation of their harmful behaviour patterns.

A narcissist might frequently make grand promises, whether in personal or professional contexts, to create an image of reliability or generosity. However, when they inevitably fail to deliver on these commitments, they won't take responsibility. Instead, they might blame external circumstances, or worse, other people. They might also claim that someone else's actions prevented them from fulfilling their promise.

This evasion of accountability not only shields the narcissist's self-image but also confuses and frustrates those around them, creating a dynamic where the narcissist is never at fault.

Over the years, I got used to Ian telling me that he planned to do or to buy something for me but didn't. Unsure of how to respond, especially if I needed to hide my disappointment if it was something I really wanted or needed; I turned the incident into a standing joke by saying with a smile,

"Oh, just another prize I could have won, but didn't"

He would respond with,

"Something like that," and smile.

And that would be the end of that conversation. However, what was notable is that the prizes I never won ended up being less extravagant but would have been, if given, more emotionally affectionate. Such as,

"I was going to buy you roses for our wedding anniversary but didn't."

Or he would sometimes change it around to,

"I wanted to buy you some perfume, but the store only had cheap stuff, like…" He would then name something he knew that I liked. Quite often, anything I chose for myself he disliked.

It's not so much that I wanted the gifts, unless it was something I really needed; but it was just yet another mind game, where he controlled whether a special event could be celebrated or marked by the giving of something.

    I know that the Christmas season can be a difficult time for many. However, for some reason, I love Christmas, but I've no idea why, because I can't say that the day has ever lived up to expectation. But deep down, I'm a bit of an old romantic and I love Christmas trees and fairy lights, watching traditional movies with a glass of fizz and a box of chocolates. I love the romantic notion of family and friends coming together. I love the stories within traditional hymns that speak of a baby being born in a manger; the guiding star that brought exotic travellers to visit with gifts.

Needless to say, Ian hated Christmas, so when it was just the two of us, it got cancelled. Instead, we'd go for one of his infamous long drives and I would stare out of the car window; see houses with trees and decorative lights, people arriving with gift boxes. Families and friends, hugging on doorsteps.

There was never any give or take in my relationship with Ian; every day was designed around his needs or his mind games. As a result, he used Christmas as just another means to justify his warped logic. He would claim that if the event couldn't live up to his personal grandiose ideals, then it wasn't worth celebrating.

Therefore, if we couldn't afford to stay at a 5-star luxury hotel for Christmas or New Year, then we didn't celebrate. He cared very little if at all, for how his attitude affected those around him and seemed totally oblivious to the fact that these events are about people and not how much it costs. Thus, even when Lauren was still living at home, while I'd insist on a tree and presents, Christmas day would invariably be spent on a road trip.

Likewise, Ian's viewpoint enabled him to blame others for his lack of money. I suspect also, that having limited resources meant that he could no longer present gifts as a grand gesture to impress guests. While I appreciated the beauty in some of the grand gifts Ian presented me; if the presents had been given out of true love, rather than a grandiose routine of 'look at me', he would have known that I believed that less is more.

To everyone on the outside, Ian appeared to be really charming, successful, and spontaneous. They didn't know the precarious, self-serving, manipulative, and controlling man, who did little to protect or safeguard our interests. Behind his ongoing grandiose façade, I learnt that Ian had an even bigger catalogue of failed business ventures that spanned decades. This only came to light when we were eventually forced to sell the house we called home, in Devon.

Seemingly after leaving the military, he went into trading and merchant banking; he claimed that he was the top salesman, which meant that he had access to money. And yet, he had nothing to show for it, which he blamed on other people not known to me. He stated that his intellectual property had either been stolen or someone had ripped him off and left him with nothing. He claimed that this was why he went into business with his brother, Paul; because even though they didn't really get along, he asserted that at least family could be trusted.

Thus, years before we met, Ian and Paul had tried to launch numerous businesses that ranged from eco-solutions, funding off-shore treasure hunts to producing dog food, before settling on the more recent trading platforms. Again, the previous businesses that had failed, hadn't failed because of bad luck or anything Ian had done; but had failed because, everyone and everything else was to blame.

When it came to focusing on the new trading venture, Ian ensured that he had nothing to do with the paperwork or finances, which meant that he couldn't be held accountable if anything went wrong. Ian's role was to find a suitable trading platform and to source investment clients. This left Paul responsible for the day to day administration of the platform and clients. If the client fell through, Paul would be blamed for lacking in people skills. If the trading platform turned out to be untrustworthy, then Ian would blame Paul for not doing his due diligence. All Ian wanted to do was wine and dine potential traders and clients, but not actually get involved in the process of ensuring that the people in question were honest and legitimate.

I lost count of how many court actions were either being taken out against Ian and Paul's company or them taking action against someone else. The list was endless. They literally lost millions of pounds of client money via untrustworthy trading platforms. The situation got so bad, that I once sat down with Ian's son Ollie and showed him what I'd managed to find on the Internet regarding one so-called trader. Both the trader and his father had served time in prison for fraud. This prompted Ollie to research another trader who the company had dealt with and lost money, but instead of finding that the guy was a professor of maths as stated, he'd been a carpet salesman. If the two of us, Ollie, and I, could find this information so easily then why wasn't Paul and especially Ian, who made the connections, doing the same.

Eventually, Ian appeared to strike gold with a trader working from mainland Europe; he seemed very legitimate. However, about a year into the trade, concerns were raised regarding the trader when a member of staff began to express their worries, which related to how the trader was operating and also, Paul's misuse of company funds. So, even when a member of staff bravely highlighted that there was a very serious issue within the company to Ian, he failed to challenge his brother. His attitude was that it wasn't his problem because he wasn't responsible for the administration. Ian's inactivity and lack of accountability resulted in the company, and more importantly, to clients losing millions.

Ian's lack of responsibility affected his relationship with his son Ollie, who was employed by the company until it collapsed. Ollie pleaded with his father to do something to challenge Paul and for them to take action to protect the company and client funds, but Ian didn't see it as his problem, he wasn't to blame. Speaking out was confessing that a problem existed.

Beryl had invested in the company and had released equity on her home of 60-years to support her sons; between Ian and Paul, they were meant to pay back the equity so that her house could stay in the family. Instead of paying her back, both of them prioritised living a lavish lifestyle. As Beryl aged and the confusion of old-age set in, she often spoke of her wish to leave her coastal home for family to enjoy. She believed until her death that her wish would be granted; she was unaware that when she died, her home would be sold to clear the equity debt.

At no point, did I sense any genuine remorse from Ian; he would say all the right things regarding how bad he felt about his mother's predicament, while at the same time, blame Paul and everyone else for the financial demise.

There are certain traits I don't doubt that Ian learnt from early childhood. While his mother Beryl would always state that Ian was her preferred son, she generally lacked any true affection for anyone. She often played her sons off against each other, and while in adulthood, Ian and his brother were business partners, there was always a jealousy surrounding Beryl's proclaimed feelings for Ian. Thus, Ian and Paul had a general dislike for each other; beyond work they never socialised. When we lived in Devon, Paul lived less than ten miles from us, but we never visited his home.

As a result, Beryl was often the source of any rifts they had, primarily regarding favouritism. If Ian was the preferred younger son, Paul often used this as an excuse to wash his hands of any responsibility for his mother's well-being in later life.

Likewise, Beryl viewed me as her biggest competition for Ian's affection. She had a very sharp tongue and would often leave me in tears; Ian said nothing to protect me.

What was evident within this family, between Beryl, Paul, and Ian, is that they all treated other people as though they were in service to them. What appeared to be generosity, for example, receiving money for running a 'family' errand, would always turn out to be a form of control. It always felt that any payment made for petrol or time, was given so that you would end up being indebted to them. This meant that they could always call upon you at any time, to have or get what they wanted. If you were unable to jump when instructed to do so, each dealt with their prey in individual ways.

With Beryl it would be a vicious tongue lashing of name-calling; from Paul, he would use his great mind to devise legal threats; as for Ian, it was covert psychological abuse. Between them they were a toxic trio and yet, they publicly portrayed a union of pride in protecting and living up to their family name. Nevertheless, Ian and Paul, had one grandfather who apparently lost his money on horses, cars, and women; the other beat their father.

What became clearer toward the end of our relationship is that Ian liked to hide behind women and claim that he was doing it for their benefit. He used his mother's address throughout his entire adult life, even though he'd been married twice, and, on both occasions, the marital home had belonged to his wife. Likewise, utilities were in Jane's name for years after their relationship ended, and when I arrived on the scene, transferred to me.

On paper, Ian didn't own anything, but would claim that everything belonged to him. It was as if he wanted or needed to be invisible or simply unaccountable. Yet behind closed doors, he wanted to be the puppet master, but for no one externally to know just how much he was really in control. By placing everything in my name, he tied me into the relationship, which also allowed him to hide behind me, even to the extent of running up debt and using bank cards in my name. When I showed signs of distress and questioned what was actually in place to protect me long term, Ian would accuse me of either not supporting him or lacking in a vision for the long term plan. The realisation that Ian liked to hide behind the women in his life, made me feel vulnerable; I suspected that he was more than capable of throwing me under the bus to protect himself. The man in shining armour was no Knight!

So, when our lives began to unravel and the business venture started to collapse, we had no savings due to Ian having spent most of his earnings during the good season, on cars, artwork, and expensive rental properties. I was grateful that we still had our base in Devon, but with no savings, we relied on selling Ian's extravagant assets to fund our basic needs. While this was financially helpful at first, it still had a natural lifespan. Therefore, even though I was able to return to work, my earnings weren't enough, long-term, to meet the cost of our basic outgoings. Over time, we would use up the money raised from selling cars and artwork and would be running at a deficit every single month.

To avoid this scenario, I came up with an idea of how to resolve the situation. The idea was to sell the house to release the equity and combine that with the funds raised from the sale of assets, to buy a smaller house, in a more affordable area of Devon. I had secured work with the local council and therefore, my role was highly transferrable. I even went as far as researching what could be bought with the money and what job roles were available; and the options were pretty good. Not lavish, but comfortable and safe.

But Ian was having none of it. In fact, he got very nasty, to the point of threatening. I was told that under no circumstance was I ever going to tell him how to live his life. I was reminded that while I was used to less and that basically, the kind of person who could be happy doing my 'little menial council job' that was never going to be him. And again, if I didn't like it, I knew exactly where the door was. The threat was so menacing that I was too scared to remind him that legally, I was the registered owner of the property and had been for 20 years.

After the threat, I was plunged into days of silence. I was dependent on him to drive me to and from work; sometimes he would and sometimes he wouldn't. However, thankfully, I could walk to work in just under 40 mins if needed. The third party mind games, and the comparisons to Eva and Noelia, got worse. It felt that this was his way of blaming me for all the things he no longer had in his life; therefore, if I had been more like Eva, we would be living off my high salary or living in Paris with affluent, influential friends, and holidaying in Mallorca. But what did I have to offer, nothing!

During my weekends off work, he would still take me on erratic drives across the moors, challenge me to drive home knowing full well that I couldn't. We visited luxury hotels where he would buy us one cup of coffee each and we would make it last for hours; he'd smoke cigars bought for him by his mum.

What is sad, is that even though I feared Ian, I still felt wretched for him. I felt like I was witnessing the demise of the character Willy Loman in Miller's *Death of a Salesman*; Loman is a delusional fabulist, whose self-perpetual denial affects everyone around him. But even in the play, there is a reckoning of accountability; but not for Ian, he was blameless.

Nonetheless, not taking action to safeguard what little funds we had inevitably saw them slowly disappear; it was only a matter of time before our world would completely crash. Behind this was the stress of legal action against Ian and Paul's company.

Ian hung onto the home in Devon for as long as he could, until resources had almost gone. At that point, his anger was explosive, and he hit out in all directions; the behaviour patterns excelled to some horrendously low, painful, and demeaning insults. Nonetheless, he eventually had no choice but to agree to selling the house. We were completely dependent on whatever equity could be raised to assist us in starting over. I was still tentatively encouraging the mindful track of downsizing and transferring my council job, especially as I was doing really well in my role, but Ian adamantly disagreed with this idea.

In his opinion only his drive for billionaire success was ever going to save us, so he stated that it was his way or no way, I knew the way to the exit. If the usual pattern of showing me the door wasn't enough, he added the additional layer of guilt tripping by reminding me that it wasn't his fault that we were in this mess; he was simply the victim.

Eventually the house sold, which had been home to Ian for four decades and in my case, perhaps the most permanent place I'd lived, albeit on and off, for 20-years. It was a place that had felt like home when permitted.

On Ian's instruction, we left Devon for the southeast in early 2000; we moved into a temporary 3-month rental. The plan was for him to go back into the city to make more contacts so that he could rebuild a business; he already had a few ideas in the air and saw it as something that would progress quickly. This meant that the first rental accommodation, a stable block, was to be temporary, as he planned to move into something more suitable.

Again, I was discouraged from seeking work; reminded that my skills were out of date and that the cost of getting me to work, would negate my earning potential. However, slung into what felt like last chance saloon, I ignored Ian's advice and began secretly exploring my employment options. I needed to believe that if we both worked hard enough, that it was possible to start over again. Then COVID hit and the entire world came to a crashing halt. Our problems suddenly became much bigger than just us and if we were to stand a chance of surviving, then the odds that we felt were already stacked against us, were changing by the second because of a global pandemic that hit the pause and reset button on how humanity would operate moving forward into the future.

As a result, any hope that I felt we had moving forward, suddenly felt impossible. We would be attempting to re-enter a world that already felt was full of obstacles due to age and dated skillsets. So, like countless people, all around the world, it felt like that even if we were to survive an epidemic, that we would be on the bottom of the pile when it came to seeking a place within new ventures or careers.

Once more, money was fast disappearing. We were living off the equity from the sale of the Devon house, which had incurred other costs, including legal fees and bills for the storage of furniture and furnishings. The cost of rent and utilities was almost double the cost of living in Devon. COVID also meant that we couldn't retrieve our belongings from storage, therefore, we were short of clothing and some home essentials. Outings to the supermarket became a regular regulated trip; I remember the judgemental stares of purchasing underwear, bedding, or an ironing board: to many these were viewed as none essential items, but everyone's story was different, and this was often forgotten in a world that had been side-swiped.

Nonetheless, Ian came up with an alternative plan, which was to place the equity raised from the sale of the house onto his latest sourced trading platform. I cried; it felt like he hadn't learnt anything from the fallout of his past failed endeavours. But he was adamant that we had no choice; once more it was only a matter of time before the money would run out again, and this time, we would have nothing left, no assets whatsoever, to bail us out. So, he did it, he put the remainder of our funds onto a trading platform.

As expected, the dividends began to be paid, but it was a matter of knowing for how long; and finding out whether we would get the initial investment back as agreed. In fake schemes, known as Ponzi Schemes, the set-up is to pay investors from a non-existent enterprise with the funds collected from new investors; if these dry up, so do the dividends.

So as soon as COVID restrictions were relaxed a little and we began to receive dividends Ian wanted to move to a new rental property, one that was much bigger and grander, than the temporary residence. So, the phone calls to letting Agents began, as did Ian's banter to talk about how he was a wealthy man seeking to decide where he wanted to put down his roots. He offered the narrative that he wanted to rent before he decided to buy; he claimed that his budget was limitless. He requested that his new home needed to be big enough to house his artwork and selection of cars; all of which, in reality, had been sold to survive.

Thus, the cycle was starting all over again. But of course, none of it was Ian's doing, he was just the victim of everyone else's failings, including mine.

'Accountability requires honesty, integrity, vulnerability, and courage. Don't expect any of these qualities from narcissists. They cannot hold themselves accountable for their actions. To do so, requires owning up to the fact that they have flaws and make mistakes.'

[Copyright: FreedomFromNarcissisticAndEmotionalAbuse]

9

Red Flag: Lies

    Consistent dishonesty is a key trait among narcissists. Recognising these narcissist red flags is essential for self-protection. From minor details to significant matters, they weave a complex web of deception that's hard to untangle. This constant untruthfulness creates a fog of confusion and mistrust, leaving you unsure of where you stand. It's a manipulative tactic designed to keep you off-balance and questioning your own judgement. It also conveniently obscures the narcissist's true intentions or actions, making it harder for you to hold them accountable or challenge their behaviour effectively.

    It's difficult to know where to start on the subject of lies especially when advised by two professionals that my entire relationship with Ian was based on them. Clearly, there were elements of his life that were difficult to hide, such as his family dynamics, which meant that I witnessed these physical truths. However, the definition and extent of his lies, as advised, would always be orchestrated to ensure that he maintained control to always benefit himself fully.

On an emotional level Ian was basically telling me what needed to be said to ensure that I remained tethered to him. But instead of filling me with lies regarding how much he loved me or how attractive he found me, he instead, used indirect reverse psychology to belittle my self-esteem and self-worth, so that I truly believed in the lies that I was unlovable and unwanted; that I needed his love, no matter how warped, to exist.

Thus, Ian was a man who deliberately and systematically chose to destroy qualities within me to maintain control; which is how twisted the lies can become. To get me to believe in those lies, he manipulated my weaknesses, which were empathy, people-pleasing, fear of confrontation and abandonment. I was also deeply traumatised and grieving the loss of Hugh. Therefore, as a grieving, single, plus size mother, I was a less physically and emotionally attractive option for Ian. However, my vulnerabilities and the fact that I had access to my own supply of money, made me attractively convenient in Ian's world.

I think part of the lie, also, was that Ian never really wanted a wife, he wanted a housekeeper, because if he'd really wanted a romantic spouse, a lover; someone to love and someone who made him look good, he would have opted for a trophy wife. But that would have played upon his own insecurities, because she wouldn't be lacking in confidence and that would have kept him on his toes. Therefore, he needed someone less glamorous who lacked confidence, because they could be more easily controlled.

Thus, in his mind, he couldn't have it all; so, while the trophy wife, would look the part in the grandiose showcases and have been the preferable choice in the bedroom, that would have been too high risk if he himself was insecure. Therefore, he found it preferable to make do with someone like me, Chloe, because while I may not look the part for his egocentric shows, my lowly background ensured that I would be happy with whatever scraps of joy and attention was thrown in my direction. As in childhood, he wasn't only just allowing me to eat the whole meal, I could have a seat at the table too. Plus, I was a relatively cheap date, so to speak; because not only did I initially have my own money, but my expectations were more easily fulfilled.

As for the bedroom, all he had to do was improvise. Make me feel inferior via a lack of intimacy and affection, while making sure that I knew about his more attractive conquests. Rub a bit more salt on the wounds to ensure that I felt completely substandard by constantly playing mind games that referenced the flaws of women who were similar in features to me. As a result, when there was no real warmth or tenderness shown toward me, I believed it was my fault, because I'd been programmed to believe that I was hideous and unlovable. What a fabulous plan. And it worked too.

So, as the new cycle began, we moved into yet another rental property that virtually drained the monthly trading dividend. I tried to express my fears about not putting any money away into savings; but my concerns fell on deaf ears. Ian simply told me that he'd found the perfect platform and that it was now his time to shine. Accumulate to speculate; look the part or fail. However, after the administrative problems within Ian's business, I tentatively pushed for him to ensure that we had at least, all relevant paperwork relating to the trade agreement. This was to be a private arrangement with the trader and therefore, Ian couldn't hide behind Paul to deal with all the necessary documentation.

However, Ian was reluctant to insist on the finer detail that could protect us long term. He claimed that to be so pushy was questioning the traders credibility. He also claimed that he'd been permitted on the platform as a favour from someone who worked with the trader; normally the minimum investment was more than what we could afford. Therefore, Ian wasn't willing to do what was necessary to ensure that the investment was safe by gathering the relevant documentation. I was on tenterhooks because I was terrified that we would lose everything.

Every time I tried to express my concerns; Ian's response was to portray the trader as someone we shouldn't mess with. I was told that we needed to respect his way of working and to keep our mouths shut. It was absurd. Ian handed over £150k, almost everything we had and argued that we didn't need to have a signed contract. I felt sick to the pit of my stomach and meanwhile, trouble was still brewing from the previously failed business.

I seriously began to question whether Ian's high stake lifestyle had caused him so much stress that he was beginning to lose the plot. I wasn't by any means entrepreneurial but even I could see that his actions were beyond crazy. I considered whether he was having some kind of breakdown or whether he simply had a very serious addiction to high risk strategies. Either way, it wasn't good and if I showed a fraction of doubt or concern, I would be shot down in flames and accused of lacking ambition and not trusting him. Mentally I was in decline. I decided to only speak when spoken to, to always be in agreement regardless, because I couldn't cope with the anger and put downs.

Eventually, Ian decided that to acquire the lifestyle that he wanted, he needed to make more money faster. To do so, he needed to source more clients to invest on the platform. He thought that it was an excellent USP that he had invested his own money, into the scheme; no mention of equal ownership.

He swore blind that he would never involve his brother in any future ventures but opted to introduce him to the trader for the potential of earning commission if he invested. Ian knew that Paul was good at saving money and therefore, was likely to have a substantial amount to invest. Ian also wanted to prove to the trader that he could bring suitable clients forward to the platform, which could earn him a place at the table as an official introducer.

However, once Paul was on board, he started to create problems with the trader, and they fell out, which resulted in Ian's brother launching a scathing attack; this didn't go down well with the trader and as a result, he wanted to throw Ian off the trading platform. Which if he did, it would have scuppered Ian's entire plans for the future and any chance of creating one that was secure, in a world post pandemic.

So, the only way around the problem was for Ian to grovel and to promise to bring in more clients so as to secure his own position on the trading platform. Meanwhile, legal action against his previous company was reaching new heights and Brexit was looming. So, Ian decided that we should move to Spain, where he planned for us to gain residential status; basically, he was running away to a different jurisdiction, until things blew over. He claimed that if the legal action went to court, that we stood to lose everything and that it could lead to jail sentences; this terrified me.

However, even though Ian planned to move to Spain, he still wanted to keep a rental property in the UK, so that he could regularly return for business. The concept for a UK rental property was to enable Ian to have a comfortable base to store his handmade clothing and likewise, to continue looking every inch a man of financial standing and success Yet, this meant two rental properties at the same time, thus more expense: we were going around in circles.

We moved to Spain during COVID. We travelled on the overnight ferry from Southampton to Bilbao. At the time of travelling, masks still had to be worn onboard and there were places enroute to southern Spain, where it was impossible to stop for refreshments, because the entire town or village was in complete lockdown.

It was shortly prior to the relocation that I learnt via social media that Anita was also moving to Spain. My natural reaction was to send her a PM to find out more details. This is when I learnt that weirdly, she was heading to the exact same town in southern Spain. Her departure date was exactly one month before ours; and we were both also renting our accommodation via the same Agency. So, naturally, we had a lot in common in our shared journey to become overseas residents.

However, notably, it is only in the writing of this book that I've come to realise that Anita played a bigger role than I first thought. In creating a more manageable narrative timeline she has emerged as playing an integral part in how things unfolded toward the end of my relationship with Ian. The journey to write this book, is one that is part of my own healing process, which means that there are parts to this tale that I've only come to recall the further I've walked along the pathway in my own process of self-realisation. Therefore, the more my own healing journey has evolved, the more I came to truly see that wherever there is Light, there is dark too. The more my life began to unravel, the more I could see the need for the Light of my Holy Father, and angels, to walk me through the darkness of others.

Prior to Malcolm's death, but after we had learnt of his drinking problem, Anita and I became what I would call, very close friends. I would say that Ian did too, with Malcolm. It was an unusual scenario during a pandemic and various different lockdown restrictions; people were thrown together in extremely unusual circumstances. In supporting Anita and Malcolm, both Ian and I, did invariably try to talk, beg, and plead with Malcolm to get the help he needed to stop drinking. As friends, Anita and I also confided in each other a lot.

I told her about the strange synchronicities and my sense of unease around Ian; I also mentioned Manuel Angel recognising that my body was in trauma and while I didn't mention 'sexual abuse', I did tell Anita that I thought it could be linked to the way in which Ian treated me. I referred to the constant comparisons and putdowns, which had severely affected my well-being.

I also told her about a recent event that had upset me.

When businesses had begun to reopen after the various lockdowns, Ian was desperate for a haircut as was I, to get my hair cut and coloured. So, we booked appointments with a local hairdresser, Natalie. We had only been going to her for a very short amount of time, when Natalie and I had a conversation about relationships, love, and marriage. She spoke of her husband being the greatest love of her life and then out of the blue, said something about Ian having lost the greatest love of his life.

I couldn't believe it. I'd been with Ian for 20-years, and still, no matter where we went and who we talked to, he had to make sure everyone knew that he was used to better; a more superior home, car, lifestyle, and partner. I know that this sounds like sour grapes, but seriously, after two decades, he was telling a complete stranger the same story he'd told every letting or estate Agent, every car salesman, every business acquaintance, every new friend, including Anita and Malcolm, and anyone we met at social gatherings.

In reality, I know it wasn't about Eva as in the actual person, but more about what she stood for, or at least, what he purported she represented. It was her prestige, her earnings, her contacts, her links to Paris and Mallorca. Likewise, it wasn't grief that created the talk, it was part of the 'great I am' and 'I'm used to better' conversation.

Anita was appalled and she seemed to understand why I was upset, which was because, no matter how much I'd loved Ian, and how many years of my life I'd given him, I still didn't feature in his list of greatest assets.

In exchange for listening to my woes, Anita shared some of her own feelings. She was obviously distraught that Malcolm's drinking was causing him to decline quickly; he became wheelchair bound and needed assistance to use the bathroom. Anita was unable to help him 24/7, so they used the services of a local care company, to assist for a few hours each day.

Malcolm was unable to hold a glass and resorted to drinking from a plastic beaker with a spout. There were numerous conversations between everyone who was involved in his care as to whether or not they should continue to serve him alcohol. The general consensus was that he was at the point of no return, therefore, the decision was made to give him what he wanted in the final weeks of his life. However, while Anita was able to have a public face that suggested that she was coping, she shared that beneath the surface she was really angry with Malcolm.

In her opinion, she'd never signed up to watch her husband drink himself to death. As his body went into shutdown, she was mad too that he had chosen drink over life, especially as they were supposed to be doing the new life in Spain together. It was painful for her to know that he chose drink over her and in doing so, it was left to Anita to sort out the legalities of his imminent death, while being the one who also had to assist him in the middle of the night to get to the bathroom. I really did understand her anger, even when she wished him dead, because she couldn't stand the pain of watching him turn into a dribbling drunk.

However, what sticks in my mind, is a strange conversation, I had with Anita. She told me that she'd spent days screaming at Malcolm, telling him that he was useless, and that she would be glad when he was dead because he was a rubbish husband and crap in bed too. Again, I could totally understand her raw anger, but at no point did she ever express to me feeling any remorse for losing her temper with her dying husband. Instead of regret, she blamed her outburst on demonic possession. I did a double-take because I obviously thought I'd heard wrong; but she repeated the claim. It was such a random and crazy thing to say; but I brushed it off thinking that although she was using somewhat dramatic terminology, I could see that she was upset.

A few days passed and Anita seemed to be quite chirpy, but Malcolm was in a low mood, which was understandable. He was in a lot of pain, drinking and falling asleep, so not always fully cognisant. During these low moods, Malcolm would often talk to himself; the mix of medication and alcohol, made his words slurred and difficult to understand. As friends, we would visit him daily, in the hope that we could help lift his mood, because sometimes he liked to reminisce about music, holidays, and happier times.

On one of the last occasions that we saw him, his mood was extremely low. I listened as Malcolm began to talk to himself about how Anita had been unkind to him. He claimed that he deserved it for what he was putting her through. But again, it was the terminology and the accusation that struck me as odd; he said that she had told him he was possessed and not in his right mind. Regardless of faith and beliefs, it felt very uncomfortable to think that a man who was drifting in and out of drunken consciousness had had this thought put into his head.

Anita also confided in me that she had met someone else. I could see that she needed love, support, and comfort, therefore, I would never judge her decision to seek what she needed to move on. David was known to Malcolm as they both played golf and were drinking buddies.

Hence, it didn't seem overly odd to Malcolm for David to be in his home, assisting Anita, with part of his end of life care: it's what friends do. Nonetheless, there were several people who realised that Anita and David were more than just friends, so they turned their backs on them because they felt that it was wrong. I stood by Anita's side and supported her, because I know that life is too short to sit in judgement on how someone chooses to deal with their grief. Needless to say, I thought we were close friends and because of that, I shared with her my concerns regarding my marriage to Ian.

Anita didn't seem to openly grieve Malcolm's death; she put this down to being able to come to terms, in advance, with the outcome. She mentally prepared herself and spoke of the process and sat with him to make his funeral plan. I saw her as being spiritually strong, but I don't think others saw her in the same positive light, especially, as the plan was to not have a funeral, which meant that family and friends were denied the opportunity to properly say their farewells.

Additionally, Anita was quite keen to speak to Ian to ask him to link her with the trader as she wanted to ensure that her and Malcolm's investment could continue after his death. Anita also told David about the trading platform and was quick to turn to Ian to privately negotiate with him whether she could have any commission for introducing her new partner to the trade. Within weeks of Malcolm's death, David had moved in with Anita and was also an investor with the scheme, which again, earned Ian and Anita a commission.

Another strange and notable occurrence at this time, was that within weeks of Malcolm's death, Anita wanted to set up a small circle to do what is called table tipping.

Over the years, I've done some quite extensive mediumship training, which as I recollect my story, it is somewhat surprising that I was able to do this with no resistance, that I recall, from Ian. He hated for me to be away from him or home. He would never directly tell me that I was not allowed to do something; instead, he would use the silent treatment, guilt tripping or twist meanings to conversations, to express his dislike.

But when it came to mediumship training, I was quite active in this world and surprisingly, Ian appeared to be quite supportive for me to develop this skill. What I do know is that Ian was never left caring directly for Lauren, but as she grew up, of course they could co-exist without my need to be with them. What confuses me, is that if I was permitted to attend this training, without any negative comeback, I cannot fully understand what was in it for him; he always had an agenda. The only thing that comes to mind is that he had a keen interest in the occult; therefore, for me to gain wisdom in this field, I feel, would surely be more of a disadvantage to him if he needed to retain control.

The reason why I started to do mediumship training is because I began to see spirits after Hugh's death. I would visit places and see memories from the past. I didn't request these memories; they just came to me and at times I would be scared because I would see things that I really didn't want to see. Ian began to research into what was happening to me and learnt that it was common for a major trauma, such as waking up next to Hugh's dead body, to trigger this ability. It was seemingly even more common for someone like me, who came from a very abusive childhood, to develop overt sensitivities.

As I write my head is buzzing with thoughts: what I'm beginning to feel here is that if Ian was able to encourage me to believe that my mind was highly sensitive and needed special care and protection, once more, he was actually serving his own twisted agenda. To encourage me to explore the spirit world, to believe that I could see and communicate with the dead, played into his narrative to raise questions about my mental well-being. I also became a kind of party trick that he could call upon when needed. He would put me on the spot to give messages to family or friends. Even his brother Paul would ring to ask me what I could tell him about other people. I played up to my own oddness to win approval, while inadvertently, serving only to deepen the hold Ian had over me to think that my brain was somehow broken.

Ironically, the training was probably the best thing I did for myself, because without learning to raise my awareness, I probably would not be here now.

Nonetheless, I'd come across table-tipping as a form for spirit to communicate with the living, during my mediumship training. The practice usually involves a group of people, who gather around the table and place their hands on the surface. Sometimes, the attendees may form a full physical connected circle, by allowing their fingertips to touch.

The leader of the circle should always work with protection, and then invite spirits and loved ones, to use the energy of the group to communicate. If spirit comes through, they can use the combined energy of the people, to connect by moving the table. Usually, the energy tips the table, hence the reason why it is called table tipping; the raised leg can then be used for the motion of tapping it against the ground to form a knocking sound. Therefore, if the circle leader establishes with spirit that when asking them questions that they can respond with for example, one knock for 'no' and two for 'yes', then the table is used for this purpose.

It was certainly a method that I didn't overly like; it requires a lot of patience and an incredible amount of trust in everyone who is sat in the circle. Even when working with protection, you are still entwining your energy with other people, while inviting perhaps an unknown spirit energy to also join the party; for me this was always a big *no no*.

Therefore, when Anita suggested that she wanted to do a weekly table tipping session, remembering that she was the person Ian had called to cleanse the Hampshire house almost a decade previously, and he'd had to step in to assist; it didn't feel right. But because Anita claimed that she was desperate to communicate with Malcolm, I agreed to do it, and so did Ian. I doubted very much that the spirit of someone who had died so recently would be able to communicate so soon, but as always, I did what pleased others over what felt right for myself.

As a result, we sat in a weekly circle with four people; Anita, Ian, and me. The fourth person was usually by invite and was someone familiar with this process. The fourth person quite often could not commit to weekly sessions or dropped out because they came to feel that something was not right within the group. It would have been preferable for the members of the circle to be more consistent because that builds up trust between the members. I too sensed that there was something very wrong about Anita's desperate need to connect with Malcolm, but I supported her needs out of friendship and an element of curiosity.

However, what unfolded over the coming weeks was surreal and it's difficult to identify, especially as I know where this story is going, to now realise whether what happened was real or at least as real as it could be in an already challenging and bizarre scenario.

I've seen and heard about people sitting in circles for weeks trying to communicate with spirit and getting absolutely nothing. We sat in our table tipping circle and there was activity from the very start. The first of the four people to sit in our group was a local medium, so it was perhaps feasible that three of the four people were strong conduits for activity to occur. But this medium, a personal friend of mine, told me that the circle made her feel uncomfortable and left after just two sittings.

After the professional medium left the group, the fourth person was made up by anyone Anita could persuade to sit with us. This included her dog sitter, her new partner David, who was frankly terrified, or her visiting family or friends. However, regardless of our combined experience, the spirit activity continued to be seemingly beyond anything I've ever seen and hope to never see again in that scenario.

Over the weeks, it seemed that everyone we knew in spirit wanted to come and chat, via the table tipping sessions; it was as if the spirit world literally queued up to speak to us. Eva came through, so did Ian's dad very briefly. Relatives and friends of the fourth person and Anita too. But what became disturbing was the frequency and force in which the spirits came, which not only included my mother, but also Malcolm and Hugh. Over the next few weeks Malcolm and Hugh would connect individually, but then they seemingly started to come through at the same time, to the point that they appeared to have formed a double act, brought together by their mutual love of music.

I know how crazy that sounds, it's something you had to witness to believe, because even in the moment, I was checking to see if anyone was manipulating the table. What is even more uncomfortable here, is that via the table, thus the concept that a spirit person was speaking through it, Hugh had a message for me, and it was,

'Get out.'

This message was repeated week after week. This was happening at the same time I was experiencing the angelic numbers and synchronicities. Therefore, internally, I interpreted the message as meaning that I needed to leave Ian. However, after the circle had ended, I was not able to tell Ian what the message had truly meant to me; instead, I told him that I thought that Hugh was telling me to get out of the circle because something was really amiss with it.

I'd shared with Anita my feelings regarding Ian. Therefore, I question, again, knowing where this story is going, whether there was any way that Anita and/or Ian could have manipulated those sessions. What is also really odd, and I get goosebumps when I even think about it; is that in all the years I'd attended medium and psychic training events, not once, had my mum or Hugh ever come through.

Mediums had been able to pick up on their cause of death and general feelings of love or lack of love, for me; but for either of my mum or Hugh to communicate with such direct velocity to the point that the table would move toward me and lean in as if hugging me: it didn't feel right, no matter how much I wanted it to be true. And how did I know that the tilting motion was to be interpreted as a hug; it was because the only voice in the room at the time, was the person running the sessions and that was Anita, who would inform me:

'Oh look, he's [Hugh] hugging you.'

Which of course, I wanted to believe, because Hugh had been the only person who'd ever made me feel truly loved.

However, the table didn't just stop at tilting into a hugging motion. Whenever, I appeared doubtful or questioning, the table would tilt and lower itself gently to the floor, then over onto its top so that the surface was in contact with the floor. The entire time, our finger-tips were in contact with the table, even when it had completely flipped, we were in contact with the table legs. From here it would spin and move around the room, at times making it difficult to keep contact as we tried to the dodge furniture. I have no doubt that the spirit world is real; I have no doubt that we can communicate with spirit. However, when working with spirit it's pure love and comes from a place of pure love; but this felt like some kind of archaic freak show.

I'm not suggesting that Anita rigged wires that moved the table as a parlour trick; I'm saying that I've no idea what was at play, but somehow that circle was used to bring forth messages that encouraged my decision to leave Ian. I don't regret my decision to leave him. I just find it very odd that in the likelihood of telling Anita as my friend, that Walt had advised me to 'get out', what was the chances of Hugh's spirit coming through to say the exact same words. But stranger things have happened; at the end of the day, I took a leap of faith to change my life because of my faith in my Holy Father and angels. But the difference is, the latter is pure love, what was occurring in Anita's house was far from that.

What feels sad and uneasy here, is the simplicity in which I would always wear my heart on my sleeve, sharing personal information; so, knowing how this story unfolds, I cannot be sure whether the circle was used for another more sinister agenda, which was orchestrated by Anita and/or Ian. Even when writing this, I had to get up and leave my desk, because internally, I was shaking and this, for me, is a sign of truth.

I'm aware that this story has no clear genre, it meanders from theme to theme, as if it lacks in direction. But it's a reflection of what life with Ian was like; it was a rollercoaster of high drama ranging from grandiose lifestyles to financial corruption; psychological sexual abuse, to supernatural fantasy.

'Constant untruthfulness creates a fog of confusion and mistrust,
leaving you unsure of where you stand…'

[Source: Unknown]

10

Red Flags: Twists Conversations / Plays the Victim / Trauma Bonding

As mentioned in the previous chapter, dishonesty is a key trait among narcissists. They are capable of weaving a complex web of deception that's hard to untangle. This constant untruthfulness creates confusion and mistrust. But you may also find, that if you are ever onto them and challenge their lies, they will twist conversations, to create more lies, to create further doubt in you, but always to benefit themselves, which is to ultimately retain control over you.

Playing the victim is also a major narcissist red flag. By adopting the role of the victim, they deflect blame, generate sympathy, and manipulate others into offering support or validation. They also manage to escape accountability for their actions. For instance, in a romantic relationship, a narcissist might twist an argument, painting themselves as the wounded party, even if they were the instigator. They use this tactic to elicit their partner's sympathy and guilt. This way they divert the conversation away from their misbehaviour and toward their partner's perceived shortcomings.

Even now, as I write this account of my life with Ian, I still find it difficult to believe that I waited 20 years before seeking help. Thus, in my case, I can only be grateful that I have my spiritual faith, but this can never be a precursor for finding the courage to share concerns or to ask for help. It doesn't matter to me whether other people share my beliefs or see my faith as a coping mechanism, what matters is the ability to connect with the Self and to listen to those niggling sensations of doubt; the feeling that something is not quite right. You are your best own intuitive guide; listen to the inner wisdom or voice, in whatever form you want to label it: God, Source, angels, the soul, higher wisdom, or simply gut instinct, just please, let it guide you. Do not allow anyone to steal decades of your life as I did.

Even though I have now removed myself from the harmful situation, I continue to be constantly guided throughout the healing process. This has led me to relate the importance of recognising trauma bonding, which I did not see for myself during the relationship, but it continues to impact me greatly on a daily basis in how I interact with others and even toward my own emotional, mental, physical, and spiritual well-being. As a result, I am constantly still seeking validation from others to know my own self-worth.

Trauma bonding can be difficult to recognise because the narcissist often comes across as charming and extremely likeable, especially in public. Therefore, because others view the narcissist in a more positive light than the victim, this further deepens the target's trauma bond as it fuels their belief that they are at fault for the narcissist's behaviour behind closed doors. The longer this continues, the deeper the self-blame goes, which allows the years to tick by as the target loses more and more of themselves.

Like myself, victims of narcissistic abuse most often don't realise that they have formed a trauma bond with their abuser, which is the reason why it is so easy to get stuck in the abusive relationship, even when there is a recognition for feeling constantly unhappy and mentally exhausted. Trauma bonding with a narcissist is a result of *intermittent positive reinforcement* by the abuser. Intermittent reinforcement is the delivery of a reward at irregular intervals, a method that has been determined to yield the greatest effect from the subject, which in my case, was encouraging me to believe that I could potentially live up to Ian's expectation of the perfect woman and be deserving of a lifestyle that would not otherwise be available to me without him. Therefore, I was jumping through hoops to make myself more loveable and even though his grandiose ideals didn't resonate with my own, I came to believe that this was my own failing. My true Self no longer mattered.

However, the subject doesn't receive a reward each time they perform a desired behaviour or according to any regular schedule, but at seemingly random intervals. This means that the narcissist alternates between manipulative abuse and love bombing, which fuels confusion and instability in their target, thus leading to the development of trauma bonding.

The more time that passes, trauma bonding with narcissists strengthens. Victims become weaker and more submissive, craving validation and approval from their abusers. Narcissists positively reinforce certain behaviours, and they do this intentionally to manipulate their victims and keep them stuck in the relationship. Thus, as the narcissist gains more control, it becomes more difficult for a person to become aware of the abuse and manipulation, leading to confusion, and cognitive dissonance due to gaslighting.

Moreover, when a person develops trauma bonding with a narcissist, they keep hoping and waiting for positive reinforcements to relieve them from their emotional suffering and the feeling of rejection. Trauma bonding caused by a narcissist, conditions people into believing that toxic behaviour is normal.

Victims of narcissistic abuse might be fully aware that they are with a toxic person. However, due to the trauma bonding with the narcissist, they become conditioned to continue forgiving them. This makes it almost impossible to leave, and they end up stuck in an abusive relationship without being able to assert solid boundaries. Believe me: this is not what a healthy and loving relationship looks like. A truly loving partner makes you feel loved, supported, and accepted throughout the relationship. Getting mistreated because your narcissistic partner has a bad mood, or because you didn't feed them with narcissistic supply is completely unacceptable.

Thus, much of what I have written about was part of the trauma bond cycle, which I have learnt has 7 stages:

i) love bombing
ii) trust and dependency
iii) criticism and devaluation
iv) manipulation and gaslighting
v) resignation and giving up
vi) loss of Self
vii) emotional addiction to the trauma bonding cycle.

This is a cycle that needs to be broken. This starts by recognising that you are in a toxic relationship and/or trauma bonding. From here, devise an exit plan. Often victims have been isolated and may find it difficult to know who to trust when seeking help. If this applies to you, seek professional help from a recognised organisation or charity that assists victims of abuse. When emotionally ready, execute the plan. Once you have left the relationship, there can be NO CONTACT including on social media: don't look, don't wonder, and don't participate.

The journey to healing takes time. This means that even as I write, the pathway back to Self continually evolves. Thus, on writing the previous chapter, lots of memories came flooding back and the more that they flowed, the more that I can see that there is no error in discernment here. I recalled one of the very first dates I had with Ian. We were alone, I think Lauren was with family. Ian took me for a long drive across Exmoor and Dartmoor; it was stunning. He took me to see a stone circle and he spoke of energy and ley lines; he talked about how everything was energy and demonstrated how it exists beyond our physical. I had no real idea what he was talking about, but he went on to speak about the soul being eternal. I didn't realise that he was exploiting my need to have a shared understanding of grief and a belief that Eva and Hugh's souls were eternal.

I was thirty-years old; he was fifty; I thought he was this cool, eccentric, knowledgeable guy who had a catalogue of fascinating stories to tell. It was part of the initial attraction.

However, after I'd moved to Devon to live with Ian, stories of this nature became more of a slow drip of information. On another trip, I learnt about how he'd been experiencing visitations from Eva; he made it sound wonderful that a dead loved one could just pop in to see you. I would be left wondering why Hugh didn't come to see me.

Another day, he would reveal that Eva's regular visits from the dead, suddenly didn't feel right to him and as a result, he'd had to call his friend Robert; his friend was a priest in a nearby town and apparently, he exorcised the house. I say 'apparently', because I would later learn, some years after the event, that the process of exorcism is very stringent. Perhaps his friend blessed the house instead, I cannot be sure; but again, this is an example of how he began to play on words to evoke the sense that something of an 'evil' nature had occurred.

Admittedly, the exorcism story was fiendish, but I was still young and in the initial stages of not expecting it to be told for any other purpose than sharing a creepy experience. But then these stories would extend into him rushing into a room to tell me that he'd just sensed something standing over Lauren while she was asleep in bed; I raced to her room to make sure that she was okay. It was after that, I started to sense a male presence in the house, I could almost hear its high vibrational hum. I felt like I was being watched. Or did I?

He was good at manipulating fear. So, I now question whether he provoked fear, knowing full well that I was still traumatised from waking up next to Hugh's dead body? Did he use the knowledge of my mum's mental ill health to destabilise me? Did he combine this information with the facts that he also knew about my own acute sensitivities that stemmed from my own childhood?

He spent hours every single day watching supernatural series and documentaries. He would talk about the role of exorcists within the Catholic church and how often it's a role that was given, not achieved; often the recipient hadn't wanted the job. My interest in angels was relatively new and I hadn't really given much thought as to whether demons existed, but he would claim that that is exactly what they wanted; for us to believe that they don't exist so that they can move amongst us without us knowing.

He would challenge my belief in angels, the source that had brought me comfort after Hugh's death, by telling me that it was impossible to believe in them without recognising the fallen angel Lucifer; this came from a man who was not religious and had never read the Bible. Likewise, he fuelled the nature of my writing to the point that even my close friend, Hazel, expressed her concerns that she didn't know where the essence of my creativity and Light had disappeared to.

Ian had told me stories about how when he was in the military he'd trained in remote viewing. A research on the subject will reveal that it's a skill explored by the CIA, and the University of Columbia explains remote viewing as, a form of Extra Sensory Perception (ESP), which is the human ability to perceive information and imagery of remote geographical targets. The report adds that advanced practitioners of the Indian Yoga system were well acquainted with what they refer to as 'Divya Drishti.'

Ian claimed that everyone he'd known to train in the field of remote viewing, were dead; that the skill had driven them crazy. He said that when he had practiced it, the experience had been so dark, that he had seen figures that he referred to as the four gatekeepers, which could be from Sanskrit terminology relating to the four gatekeepers to the entrance to the Realm of Freedom. Nonetheless, his reference to the fact that everyone else was dead, was a sign that he embellished a world of danger, whereby he was the only one with the power to survive.

It's funny how Ian also happened to be the only one who could banish the demon, from the Hampshire home, when Anita failed: an event, that allowed him to be the centre of attention, and which has another disturbing layer to the episode.

The day after Ian seemingly single-handedly drove out an evil entity, he followed some advice given by Anita, on how to mirror ill-intent back to someone who is energetically sending out bad vibes in your direction. Ian used the information toward a person whose actions triggered the start to the downfall of his business; the man died within 24-hours of unknown causes. Obviously, while the person in question did die, I recognise that this sounds far-fetched, and that the death may have been a coincidence. Regardless, there was no end to Ian's belief that he had some kind of power that could be used at will to manipulate what he wanted: claims to be able to do remote viewing and hypnotherapy were just two extensions of that ideal.

All of these stories and claims, no doubt, inadvertently increased my levels of vulnerability. I was already constantly living in a fight or flight mode, in everyday life, but this added level of twisted conversations and mind games, created a deep fear of evil energy and forms. It extensively fuelled the trauma bonding; the need and belief that I could only be rescued by Ian.

I think it's important to add that it's not my wish to make this story sound like a Dan Brown novel, as the story isn't so much about angels and demons, but the extent a narcissist will go to twist a narrative so that it becomes deeply personal to the victim to the point of destruction.

According to the Oxford University Press, the definition of 'evil' when used as a noun *'his evil deeds'*, means profoundly immoral and wicked. Alternatively, when used as an adjective, *'his struggle against evil forces'*, relates to profound immorality and wickedness, especially when regarded as a supernatural force. I used to work in media and the term 'evil' was generally always used when describing someone who had carried out an atrocious act of cruelty, usually ending in death.

It's somewhat odd that I've also known three people who referred to Ian as being 'evil'. The first was someone who used to work for Ian as a cleaner. Jill was post Vicky and pre Ginny, and she used to work for Ian at the house in Devon. She was a religious woman who attended the same church where Robert practiced: the priest, who allegedly exorcised the same house. I liked Jill and we chatted a lot about spirituality, but when she was around Ian, she acted differently, almost afraid. I used to put her behaviour down to perhaps having had a bad experience with a man. Ian had noted the same behaviour and would jokingly say to me, that she looked at him as if he was the 'devil incarnate'.

Nonetheless, Jill would leave post-it notes around our house with Biblical phrases written on them; I can't remember any of the quotes, but Ian and I weren't married at the time and so I do recall that they were in the main about living in sin.

A few years after Jill left the job, I saw her with some friends at a local bar/restaurant. Ian was stood at the bar. Jill was stood with her friends to his right; they were separated by some other people, which meant that Ian hadn't spotted her. I was returning from the toilet and stepped into the restaurant area, to see a scene that looked like something out of movie set, whereby the actors need to share disapproving stares relating to someone else in the room.

Jill and her friends were all chatting while looking in Ian's direction; their faces weren't ones of admiration but looks of disbelief. Jill hadn't seen me, so I walked back toward Ian and did a detour so that I could swoop past her group; as I reached them, I heard Jill specifically state to her friends that "there was something definitely evil about him;" I knew by their actions that they were referring to Ian.

Like a fool, I told Ian what I'd heard, after all, he was my partner and I believed that we would be together forever. The information prompted him to look toward Jill; he caught her eye, and he offered her what I can only describe as a very menacing glance.

The second person to call Ian evil was one of my own spiritual teachers, Sarah. It was Sarah who assisted me in learning how to manage my empathetic qualities and other sensitivities; she also introduced me to the idea of using angels for protection. I used to sit in Sarah's psychic development circle, and it was while in this group, I made a number of friends who I'm still in contact with some of them today. As a circle, we all became quite close friends and would occasionally invite one another to each other's houses.

However, it was evident that Sarah didn't like Ian and while she said nothing directly to me, Ian did sense her dislike, and this prompted him to be very derogatory when talking about her to me; he called her fake and claimed that she wasn't spiritually gifted. I later learnt from one of the friends, met while in the circle, that Sarah had expressed her concern about Ian's energy and once again, had referred to him as being 'evil'.

Notably, Sarah was also incredibly beautiful, tall, and slim, with long blonde hair. Ian would make comparative comments about our appearances, always in her favour, but the pay off, the reward, was that he viewed me as being more intuitive and gifted than her. She was every inch the woman that I wanted to become and no doubt, Ian knew this and played upon it. However, the need for Ian's admiration and approval sadly encouraged me to distance myself from Sarah, which pains me, but no doubt, her soul knows that I have a place in my heart in gratitude to her as one of my most inspirational teachers.

The third person to use the 'evil' term was Manual Angel; which is a strange choice of words when simply discussing the essence of someone's energy field and the fact that they were relatively unknown to each other. Likewise, with limited knowledge of the English language this is the word Manuel chose.

I've heard it said that there is no such thing as a coincidence only synchronicity, which brings me back to wondering about Anita's role in how my relationship with Ian unravelled. I think back to our friendship, when I was still with Ian, and Malcolm was in the process of dying. It was what would have been Malcolm's final Christmas and instead of fussing around her husband, Anita was placing her arms around Ian, telling him that she had an extra special treat for him; she had made his favourite dessert, sticky toffee pudding.

I think back to the day when Malcolm was sitting on their terrace enjoying the afternoon sun; he was drinking a gin and tonic from a plastic beaker, but it hadn't been touched for ages: the ice long melted. It was a day when he hadn't drifted in and out of sleep but had talked about fond memories from his youth. He'd attended university in my hometown of Leeds; studied engineering.

We discovered that one of his closest friends knew a really old friend and acquaintance of mine; how our lives had been existing at the same time in the same city. We'd been to see some of the same bands on the university campus; I was younger and attending a local college, pretending to be older than I was, so that I could earn money working in a local night club.

Our link to liking some of the same bands triggered Malcolm to give me a gift; he wanted me to have something that belonged to him. It was a WIFI speaker so that I could connect my mobile phone to it, to enable me to listen to my music. I was overwhelmed by the sentiment of the gift and the fact that it was given knowing that he no longer needed it. As he handed it over to me, he told me that I was a real life living angel, adding, "I love you duck." It was a moment of the endearment of true friendship; an acknowledgment to the hours I had sat with Malcolm talking to him about his dark moods, trying desperately to reach him; I can't profess that I was the only one to try. Malcolm was a highly likeable guy, loved by a lot of people.

Nonetheless, Anita had overheard the conversation and on the mention of me being like an angel, she derisively commented,

"Well, she's not the one cleaning you up after you've shit yourself, is she?"

The comment was painfully humiliating for Malcolm. And yet, I viewed Anita as a woman in pain because her husband was dying. I caught her later when her mood had settled and tried to laugh off Malcolm's earlier comment, saying how much he was like Hugh, even down to the colour of his hair; both of them redheads from Yorkshire, who had a love for music and comedy.

I think of the many times I would confide in Anita my feelings of insecurity and how later the same day, there would be an indirect reference to it. One such incident was I had commented to her, about my weight and Ian's lack of affection.

Later, Anita appeared wearing her swimsuit to take a plunge in their swimming pool; she made a remark about how she'd had to exchange the costume for a smaller size because the weight was falling off her since arriving in Spain. She added a criticism about Malcolm not knowing how to appreciate her sexually, claiming he was pathetic in the bedroom. More humiliation for Malcolm and too much information for us as friends.

She then slid her arms around Ian and asked whether after she'd had a swim if he would like to stay for dinner as she was making a cottage pie, another one of his favourite dishes. Just as she was sauntering off for the swim, Anita suggested to me that she would normally offer to loan me a swimsuit, but she said that she didn't think she had one in my size. Anita knew that I didn't like water and that I couldn't swim; at times, her characteristics felt like an extension of Ian.

After Malcolm's death, Ian eventually returned to the UK to deal with the ongoing heated business problems. And that is how I found myself living alone on a mountain for three months, talking to my Holy Father on a daily basis. It was during this alone time, the conversations with God and piecing together all of the synchronicities and my emotions, that prompted me to make the call to Walt. The call prompted me to devise my exit plan.

I waited until Ian returned to Spain, before I announced the frightening decision to leave him. I left our final marital home, which was the miracle mountain house, *Casa Serenidad*, discovered during the girl's only outing with Anita. Consequently, it was Anita who I told about Walt's advice to leave Ian. It was from her house that I made the initial phone call to the Spanish lawyer Fernando, who then linked me up with the psychotherapist, Maria. I would have shared the finer detail of these conversations with her too.

I'd felt it only fair that I should leave the marital home, as it was my decision to end the relationship; I even went as far as trying to end it amicably as I genuinely cared for Ian and worried about him surviving on his own. I spoke of remaining friends, and supporting him the best way I could, but my reason for leaving, I stated, was that I couldn't continue to live his high risk strategy lifestyle. I was advised by Walt and Maria, not to accuse him of narcissism; face to face, this was deemed as potentially unsafe.

Within weeks of Malcolm's death, David moved into Anita's home, and a few months later, she decided to sell the house. I joined Anita and her new boyfriend on trips to view potential new properties and was excited for both of them with their plans to make a fresh start.

For a period of time, I found myself in the bizarre situation of living separately from Ian; yet I would still meet him for coffee, or visit the marital home to collect clothes, so that we could discuss how we were going to progress forward. I'd moved into a friend's house, Dawn, in a mountain village and didn't want Ian to know where I was residing. However, I would still care enough for him, to check on whether he'd eaten and sometimes find myself joining him for dinner at Anita's place. David had replaced Malcolm, Ian, and I, were no longer together, but we were two couples that still ate and chatted together. It all felt very sad, and I really wished that it could have all been very different. Nonetheless, I truly believed that we'd remain friends and I'd be pleased for him if he met a woman who could love him and give him what he truly wanted and needed. But it soon became evident that Ian had his own agenda.

Suddenly, the monthly income that was earned from the trade stopped being paid. Ian seemed reluctant to chase the missing payment; he kept insisting that questioning the trader showed mistrust and that we needed to wait for him to sort it out. A month passed and still there was no funds. I got very anxious and told Ian that I was worried and pleaded with him to ask the trader what was happening. Over the next few weeks, Ian came back with various excuses including that the banks were getting stricter about money laundering or that the funds had got misdirected. Then another month passed, and a second payment went missing. However, Anita and David were also investors, and they were receiving their funds as usual.

Because of all the failed businesses Ian had been involved I got really scared and kept suggesting to Ian that perhaps I should go to the UK police, as the investment was held in my name. But instead of sharing my concerns, he turned nasty and started to shout at me over the phone. He told me that I was unstable and mentally unwell; he hinted that my condition was because it was in my genes. He even began to imply that my demons had returned and that they were affecting my thought process, claiming that I was paranoid and delusional.

The next day, he was back on the phone asking when I was going to go home and if I wanted to go for a drive. It was frightening. When I refused both offers, he began to shout down the phone again; once more he made references to my mum's insanity and told me that I was possessed, which was why bad things always happened to me. He even suggested that the missing funds was somehow linked to my own wickedness.

When Ian decided to return to the UK for an unspecified amount of time, I was given the opportunity to move back into the marital home, but I didn't want the uncertainty of him returning without warning or risk him using guilt tactics to get me to stay. However, I did agree to keeping an eye on the house and to possible sleepovers to ensure that everything stayed safe. I could have used this opportunity to take everything from the house that I wanted for myself, but I didn't do that, because I was naive enough to believe that a form of love existed between Ian and I, which meant that we could be reasonable and fair adults to one another. I viewed his telephone explosions as pain and anger that I was leaving him.

Meanwhile, Anita's house sold and while she was awaiting for the purchase to go through on her new property, Ian came up with a plan for her and David to move into our marital home. It seemed initially like a smart idea, but it soon turned sour when Anita and David prevented me from entering the house to remove personal items.

I was read an email sent to them from Ian, basically saying that he entrusted them to take care of his home and in his absence allowing me to enter the house, would be a breach of the agreement. I was supervised taking clothing and anything that resembled a coat or jacket, I had to prove that it was mine, by showing the dress size label to help denote that it belonged to a female. I had to also negotiate removing kitchen pottery that was gifted to me by Lauren.

It was humiliating and I could barely think straight as I couldn't stop crying. Thankfully, two friends did accompany me on the day. I was unable to retrieve my much loved books, coats and boots, items that I would need during the slightly colder, but not freezing, winter months. I truly believe that Ian used the fact that it had been him that had introduced them to the trading platform, which earned them a monthly income, to manipulate them into banning me from the house. It seemed to come more naturally to Anita, to which I said to her,

"I hope the friendship (referring to Ian) is worth it."

David seemed incredibly uncomfortable, but with his own money tied up in the investment platform and viewing Ian as not only the gatekeeper to that scenario but also their temporary landlord, it was evident that he was controlling them in the same capable way that he did me.

Ian warned me that he would never agree to a divorce or financial settlement. He told me that I was worthless and that I'd get nothing from him and yet, there was very little to be had because most of it had been lost when the Devon house had to be sold. Notably, he states, I'll get nothing from 'him', which is the same arrogance endured for 20-years, that suggests that I played no part in building the life we had. He also insisted that he would wait until he was a millionaire at which point, he planned to use Paul McCartney's lawyer to destroy me.

I know that it's common for couples to get into a dispute when there is a breakdown in a relationship. But with someone who has narcissistic qualities, they don't go through the usual process of upset, anger, remorse and then find a place where negotiation is possible; they simply go into anger and destruction mode, because they have lost control of their 'victim'. This makes it additionally awkward to negotiate terms when the partnership fails.

I lost friends due to my decision to leave Ian. I heard feedback regarding his story, which was one that accused me of leaving him for dead in the water. He claimed that he was the victim and that I'd used him to benefit myself. In other stories, I was mentally unstable and an unsafe person to be with. Yet the reality is that his actions left me living in Spain, with no income, no job, no home and unable to easily seek work due to the language barrier. I was denied access to collecting personal belongings and some essential clothing.

Ian left behind the HP car, which became a cost to me, but it was essential to have transport. I was left without healthcare, which impacted on my dental and eyecare; I'm very short-sighted and suffer with eczema, so this has been hugely problematic for me.

I tried to seek further help in both the UK and Spain, and other than what friends were able to assist with, I failed on all accounts. While the Spanish legal system recognised that I was a victim of psychological abuse and financial strangulation, nothing could be done against Ian due to living in different countries. Every lawyer that I contacted in the UK could not help unless I was able to offer a down payment. I reported my case to the UK police, but again, due to jurisdictions, no one was able to help. I even called the British Embassy in Spain. It appeared that no one could help and that certainly, without wishing to enter into politics, my case was made worse because of Brexit and no one seemingly knowing whose responsibility I came under.

Ian began to barrage Lauren with unsuitable phone calls and images. One minute he would be telling her that he had no place to live and that he was sleeping in his car. The next, that he was with friends enjoying a party in 5-star luxury. He would send photographs to her of his supposed new girlfriend; the woman in question would look very young, early-twenties. Lauren suspected that he was sending random pictures of girls that he'd found on the internet, as he would never be in the photograph. She would get upset that her father figure, Ian, seemed oblivious to the affect that claiming he liked women her age was unsettling for her.

He also started to play mind games with Lauren; he would call her to wish her a happy birthday, and then do it again a week later, and again, a few more weeks later. He would then make claims that he was going senile and not in a good place. He also spoke about me in an extremely derogatory manner when talking to her on the phone; she was forced to send him an email in which she stated that she cared for us both, and that she would appreciate him not speaking about me in such a negative manner.

He also sent her a message that said something along the lines of, if he was to sit on the riverbank long enough, that he would eventually see the dead bodies of his enemies floating past. This prompted Lauren to ring me urgently because she thought he'd done something terrible to me; she later permanently blocked him. I believe what Lauren was referring to, is a quote by Sun Tzu as,

'If you wait by the river long enough, the bodies of your enemies will float by.'

Sun Tzu lived during the Eastern Zhou period (771-256BC). He was a Chinese military general, strategist, philosopher, and author. He is credited as writing *The Art of War*, which interestingly also has the following quote,

'The supreme art of war is to subdue the enemy without fighting.'

I can only wonder whether I was indeed the enemy in Ian's mind; easily subdued without actual fighting. Nonetheless, I was astounded by his capability to attempt to use philosophy to support his case and to cling onto his seat of righteousness.

Anita and David eventually moved out of the marital home; I later learnt that they'd split up and Anita had returned to the UK. I was informed by a contact that Ian had emptied the entire contents from the marital home and taken everything with him. I also heard that both Ian and Anita are now living in the same area of the UK that they initially met. I suspect that Ian and Anita are now together; whether planned or fate, platonic or romantic, is of no importance to me, because after 20-years, I am free to be me.

'The Lying Narcissist: One of the most difficult things to deal with after breaking free from a narcissist is sitting around and trying to figure out what else they lied to you about. The truth is, you'll never be able to determine what was fact, what was fiction and what was somewhere in-between. It doesn't matter, because even if you were to produce evidence of their deception(s), they will deny, deny, deny.'

[Source : @healing.after.a.narcissist]

11

TWO YEARS LATER

The Journey to I AM: an Awakening

Eleven is the ultimate, highest vibrational angelic number. Thus, I wish I could take the credit for this book having 11 chapters in total, but I cannot. It's just another magical synchronicity that keeps on happening time after time.

The journey to reach the two year point hasn't been an easy one: I would say that the hardest part of this has been the battle I've had with myself; the struggle to rediscover and redefine who I AM when I am not living beneath Ian's shadow.

For the first six months after leaving Ian, I experienced what was an all-consuming fear that made me feel physically sick to the pit of my stomach. In the darkness of the night, I would lie in bed unable to sleep, listening to the silence. I would worry about what would happen if I ran out of money; I was living on savings I'd managed to squirrel away. I'd also not contemplated Ian's reaction to attempt to destroy me. I worried about being homeless and contemplated how long I could survive living outdoors. I calculated that I would not last for long. I decided that death was preferable to not having anywhere to live. I would then lie awake thinking about how I would end it; question if I had the guts to do it if needed.

I would then sob my heart out, feeling such a deep pain of loneliness and despair that my life was so far off the track I imagined it would be. I anticipated family, friends, and a sense of home and belonging. I had none of these things and the feeling of aloneness was like falling into a deep soundless abyss, where my cries couldn't be heard.

I would fall asleep eventually and then wake up feeling exhausted, note the same empty silence and fears of being homeless; thoughts returning to how I could end it all. Then sadness and fear all over again. I felt like I was suffocating, as if someone had cut off my oxygen tank.

Sleep rarely brought any comfort or rest. I was plagued by the most horrendous dreams; the kind of dreams that felt real, as if I'd had a visitation in the night. In the first dream, it was like a dream within a dream. In the dream I woke up from a dream and saw that my bedroom door was closed. From beneath the door, I could see a pair of feet, which I knew belonged to Ian. It felt like the door was keeping him out and the feeling of the dream was one of an evil presence. I awoke from the dream shaken and exhausted.

The next time, it was another dream within a dream; whereby I awoke and this time the bedroom door was wide open. I could feel someone in bed next to me and I turned to look; it was Ian and his face looked evil. He licked the side of my face and that is when I woke up, again still feeling fearful and mentally over-burdened with the need to survive.

A more recent dream was that I was fast asleep, when Ian jumped onto the bed and growled like an animal. Again, the dream woke me, and I was so shaken and upset, I couldn't go back to sleep. Later that morning I had a text message from an old friend called Linda.

I met Linda via Sarah's psychic development circle; Sarah being one of the people who had referred to Ian as evil. Linda is an accomplished tarot card reader and medium. At the time in which Anita used to have her esoteric shop in Hampshire, Linda ran a very similar shop in Sussex. For years, I have stayed in contact with Linda, as I have done with several members of that circle. She is not someone I speak to every week or even every month, but periodically, we touch base. I had informed Linda that I'd left Ian, but since telling her, we hadn't spoken for months. On the morning of this latest dream, she sent me a text to say that my face had appeared in her mind as soon as she'd awoken and this had prompted her to check in with me, because she felt that something was wrong.

I got in touch with Linda a few days later. I told her that her message had been timely, and about the dream. She told me that she felt that this dream was bad energy that was being sent my way; she told me to protect myself. She wasn't trying to scare me, but we understand the power of energy and intention and what it can do. She suggested that I place something of spiritual importance to me, close to my front door: we agreed that an angel would be good. She also picked up on Ian's energy and said that it wasn't very powerful, but to be careful of the woman who stood at his side. I believe that woman is Anita.

A few days after this conversation, a friend in Spain, introduced me to a man who was renovating a property to transform it into a healing centre. The idea was, that we should link up with a view to perhaps doing some work together. The property was far from complete and thus, I met him just the once, but have him in mind for future projects. However, during this visit I spoke about my love of angels, and he gifted me a small wooden angel that had been hand carved by a friend of his, who lives in Bethlehem. The angel now sits facing my front door. Once you start to see the magic, it is endless.

Yet regardless of the deep level of fear I experienced, at no point have I ever regretted my decision to leave Ian. However, I did become quite concerned that I didn't even shed a single tear of remorse. I couldn't understand how I could dismiss a 20-year relationship, with such an air of ease; I considered whether it was in fact, I, who was the cruel and cold person in our relationship. Maria, the psychotherapist, said that this was a sign that I'd simply made the right move; she advised that it is difficult to feel remorse when moving from harm to safety.

I was eventually able to move past the idea of ending my life as an option, when friends, Jilly and Nigel offered me a lifeline. They told me that if I couldn't build a new life for myself in Spain, that their home in Hampshire, was always open to me to go and live. They offered to help me get back onto my feet if need be. While I didn't really want to leave Spain, their kind offer was just what I needed to feel a sense of safety. It was a Plan B, which gave me hope and for that, I will always be truly grateful to them. These were the same friends who offered me an out from my marriage more than a decade ago. Jilly with her diamonds and choice of Range Rovers, who never, not once, made me feel less than her.

I was living in a townhouse in a mountain village rented to me by my friend; Dawn and her daughter, Natalie, were my on-the-ground and in-the-moment source of comfort and support. I could literally text them and tell them that I was in a dark place, and they'd come round to the house and sit with me. Dawn admitted that she was not big on hugs but would write me practical lists of jobs to do to help me stay focused. Dawn's husband would occasionally help with other more useful jobs such as sourcing spare gas bottles or fixing problems around the rental property.

What I did forgot during those early months was that if I could trust God to guide me to leave an abusive relationship, then I could also trust in Him to help me navigate the rest of the journey. I would spend hours each day talking to Him and the angels and at first, every conversation would come from a place of absolute fear. I needed to address all of my worries and I would literally beg Him to help me. But over a period of time, I began to realise that whatever I asked for, as long as I was requesting for something from my heart and not from a place of fear; if whatever I required served my soul's purpose, then I would invariably be guided to finding a solution to acquire what was needed for me to fulfil that function.

I live in Spain and to date, I am still learning the language. But I'm not fluent enough in the dialect to compete for job vacancies, as there is a standard requirement to speak a good level of Spanish. I really want to learn the language, but lessons cost money and I found myself in a chicken and egg scenario whereby I needed to learn to gain employment and yet, I didn't have the money to enable that to happen; it would take months if not years, to become fluent enough to improve career prospects. So, this concern was just one of the many things that kept me awake at night.

As did my legality to remain in the country. I have residential status, but without work, I had no entitlement to receive financial help. Without a job, I wasn't paying taxes or toward national insurance or a health care system. Therefore, what would happen if I became sick, because I could no longer afford to have private healthcare, which was a requirement for residential status.

However, when I turned to God and asked for him to help me find employment so that I could alleviate the fear of not surviving, a job came along. A friend of a friend mentioned that a local restaurant needed staff. I applied for the job, and I was offered work on a temporary and ad hoc basis. I was really grateful for the work, but I initially didn't get enough shifts to be able to afford to pay my rent and car lease. I needed the car to get to work.

So, once more, I thanked God for the gift of the job but suggested that I needed a full-time job that paid more money. In the back of my mind, I knew that I was being motivated by fear and that on a soulful level I needed to work in a more spiritual and holistic manner. However, another job came along, which was full-time. But the job was in a different town some distance away and I was not really confident enough to tackle the drive. Nonetheless, I accepted the post and by the end of the first week, I drove to the coastline near home and contemplated driving my car into the sea.

I was so sad. I had what I'd asked for, which was a full-time job, so that I had money, and I could pay my bills. But I was unhappy and simply not ready for such a big step. The journey took its toll on me, pushed every single anxiety button that existed within my body. To keep the job, I would have also needed to relocate to a different town, as the cost of petrol made the position not cost effective. So, I left the job. I felt terrible and ungrateful for giving up on what had felt like a divine gift.

I began again my conversations and meditations with God, which led me to realise that the reason that I hadn't felt ready to move to another town, was because I was beginning to feel safe and a sense of belonging in a place that was starting to feel like home; I couldn't leave this. I realised that behind all the mental and emotional struggle that what I actually desired was beginning to form regardless of whether I was able to see it. I was energetically shifting into I AM safe, and I AM home mode.

After this, I decided to then ask God for work that was part-time, local, and that allowed me to get paid to write. I was then offered a writing job for a local newspaper. However, the terms and conditions were really bad.

So, I was yet again challenged to be brave enough to not settle for anything that did not allow me to feel valued. I needed to learn to stop being a people-pleaser and being fearful of saying no to an arrangement that didn't feel right for me on a soul level. I started to shift into a space whereby I AM confident, and I AM worthy of being valued.

Throughout these various job opportunities, I was still doing irregular shifts at the restaurant. But even though I was spiritually growing, I was still unable to shake the fear of scarcity; not having enough money to survive. So, the next time I asked for help, I was very specific in my request to God of what I wanted. I even named my price; I told Him I needed 2,000 euros a month to rebuild my life adequately and to negate all my fears regarding lack.

Once more, I was offered a job, working as a sous chef at one of the region's top restaurants. Against all the odds, age, fitness, and experience, I was selected for the post. The salary was fantastic. After the second day, the chef, who was also my boss, wanted to increase my salary as he felt that he'd found his perfect sidekick.

However, this time, I was working with a man who believed it was okay to scream at me throughout the shift. None stop yelling that made me so nervous, that I began to make stupid mistakes. If I messed up, I was sent out of the kitchen to stand alone in the green room. I had to do the walk of shame past all the diners and other work colleagues, who offered pitiful stares.

I worked crazily long hours with a man who encouraged me to believe that with him, I could rebuild my life, buy my house, my car and have everything I'd ever wanted. The price was to have him yell and call me names. I was called a 'lump' and an 'imbecile.' He made references to my sous chef abilities as 'housewife' standard. Yet, within two weeks I was back sitting in my car, staring out to sea, and contemplating ending my life again.

Once more, I turned to God to guide me. I felt terrible that everything that I appeared to want and need, against all the odds, kept landing in my lap. I couldn't understand why I felt so unhappy, and it was then that I realised that the chef's treatment of me, had echoes of everything I was running away from with Ian. My unhappiness in relation to the chef was a reaction to the overt bullying that formed part of the chef's popularity complex. I was an unsuspecting participant of his show; an unintentional verbal punchbag that allowed him to play out some kind of Gordon Ramsay wannabe fantasy. It kept the diners entertained; made the restaurant popular not only for its genuinely good food, but for the hot tempered chef.

For some keen upstart, this may have been acceptable; not that I condone bullying, but if someone was able to play along with the 'act' it could work. But for me, it just triggered fear and anxiety, the sense of not being good enough. It didn't matter to me that at the end of the shift the chef would always offer me a fist punch and tell me that we made a great team. I realised that no amount of money was worth revisiting the feeling that I would always be seeking the chef's approval, waiting for a compliment and a moment to know that I was doing good: I'd just escaped another form of this with Ian.

So, once more, I left another job. I realised at last, that allowing myself to be motivated by the fear of scarcity was never going to bring me happiness or fulfilment. I spent a lot of time meditating and speaking to God about my fear of scarcity and I found myself recollecting memories from my childhood and previous relationships. My parents never had any money. They lived in fear of final bills and a knock on the door from the debt collector; as a child I got used to hiding behind the sofa with my mum when someone came asking for payment.

It was a household that taught me as a child not to dream big because people like us, working class, could never be successful. We were born to struggle and to be broke our entire lives. I'd come home from school to an empty fridge and nothing to eat. Mum would blame my dad because he was a great car mechanic, everyone liked him; but he was useless at asking for payment. My mum's generation had believed that her role was to marry and provide their husband's with children; in return the husband would take care of her financially.

There appeared to be no lesson on what to do if the husband failed to do this. Turn to other family? But if they didn't exist either, then what? No one seemed to have any answers to these questions. My mum was unhappy but stayed because there was no route out for her, until another man took over my dad's role. My parents encouraged me to believe that my life had the same destiny, that I needed a man to exist in this world. No one told me that I had the capabilities to do it myself.

I married Mac at the age of 17 and he'd grown up in a similar family environment. He'd not suffered cruelty, but he was certainly brought up surrounded by financial scarcity. His parents were broke, and their situation worsened during the 1980's coal miners' strikes. Mac joined the military as a teenager with a wish to travel and to live a different kind of life. But our life together saw us trapped in a cycle of needing bank loans to meet basic costs.

It all started with an accidental overdraft, which we were unable to pay back until our next pay cheque. I remember the bank manager advising us to take out a small bank loan to cover the overdraft, which would enable us to pay it back in instalments, rather than the whole lot getting swallowed up in one payment, leaving us short of money again. We took out the loan, but as soon as we needed something else, such as repairs to the car, or a trip to the dentist, we'd then struggle to pay for these in addition to the loan. Hence, it was just easier to keep extending the loan; getting a loan to pay off another loan to have more money in our hands.

Follow this with 20-years of Ian's lifestyle whereby no amount of money was ever going to be enough; therefore, it seemed inevitable that I would have a negative relationship with money. I learnt that my fear of financial scarcity was a learned behavioural pattern that stemmed back to my childhood. Therefore, I had to learn that I AM financially abundant.

With another job not working out for me, I called my boss at the previous restaurant to tell her what had happened; I asked if I could be considered for any available shifts, which she agreed to. It turned out that in the short time I'd been away there had been some staff changes, which meant that more shifts would be available. The timing was perfect. So, I returned to the restaurant, which sits in the mountains with views of orange, lemon, and olive trees. My boss, a female, Carola, is younger than me, but has over the past two years, become a very close friend.

She offered me work regardless of my age and my ability to speak Spanish. I am now employed on a contract, which affords me access to the healthcare system and sees me as contributing to the local economy, which is good for me long-term in making Spain my home.

When I'm not at work we check in with each other most days; we talk of men and love and dreams. We laugh a lot and have the same quirky sense of humour. To me, she's a young mum and at times, I feel that my role is somewhat maternal when needed: a sharing of wisdom, for what it's worth, having worn the t-shirt some decades in advance. In return, her fiery, no nonsense, Latin blood, teaches me to go with the flow and to not over think things.

Like Dawn and her family, Carola, never allows me to spend Christmas or birthdays alone. My first Christmas post Ian was spent with Dawn, Natalie, and their family; they also took me out for lunch on my birthday. Now that I'm at the restaurant, I work on Christmas Day, but the following day, we gather at Carola's house for a banquet of food.

Carola has been the chef of her own restaurant for many years and it's a homely place that is frequented by many of the locals. Thus, it's a job that has enabled me to not only earn an income but has placed me in the heart of a community. I literally cannot go anywhere without someone waving or saying hello, which I appreciate.

With an income I was able to begin to stabilise mentally and emotionally. I began to find joy in the simple things of life. I started to do small things for myself, such as take a drive to the coast for a walk and then breakfast. I needed to see the sea, to begin to enjoy the landscape rather than viewing it as a place to end it all. More and more timely synchronicities continued to come my way, which allowed me to feel strongly connected to God and to trust in Him to assist in my healing journey and guidance to fulfil my soul purpose.

One day I saw a post on Facebook advertising a talk on the subject of self-love, which was to be held at a seafront café. I felt inspired to attend as I thought I may find the talk useful, and it was a chance to potentially meet like-minded people.

The talk was well presented by a couple called Jonas and Clare. After the event, which was attended by a dozen people, many of us stayed over to enjoy a coffee and to chat further. To my astonishment Jonas had been a fellow student of Sarah, whose circle I had sat in in the UK.

In addition to Sarah's psychic development circles, she was also a very accomplished angel teacher and energy healer; Jonas had also been one of her clients. Learning this, led to a conversation about the training I'd received from Sarah and how I'd too explored various forms of energy healing. Jonas told me that both he and Clare had wanted to find a wonderful local energy healer and asked whether they could have an appointment with me. Brushing aside any doubt, I trusted in the synchronicity of our meeting and nervously accepted them both as clients.

A week later, Jonas and Clare came to my house for an energy healing session. I was terrified. I hadn't done energy healing for years; I felt like a fraudster. I was guided to trust and to set my intention and to work from a place of unconditional love, and that is exactly what I did. I used everything I'd ever learnt over the years from teachers and readings and my trust in God.

After the session, Jonas told me that he could tell that I was one of Sarah's students; I carried the same Light and that I was doing God's work. It felt somewhat egotistic to allow his feedback to mean something to me, but it did; but only from the sense that I needed to know that I was right in trusting and not heading toward insanity.

Jonas and Clare became regular clients. They shared the same love in their faith of a God, and it was a comfort to have someone to share my spiritual beliefs and healing gifts with. As our friendship grew, it became evident to them that I still had some fears relating to scarcity and it was Jonas who introduced me to *The Abundance Book* by John Randolph Price; this book was literally God-sent. It's a very small book that contains 10 valuable lessons, and it really helped me to begin to realise that I could truly create a beautiful, abundant, purposeful, and soulful future for myself.

The extra income I earned from offering healing sessions to Jonas and Clare, allowed me to further my training and to explore dormant spiritual interests. I wanted to learn an energy healing modality that was recognisable to most people. I trained to do reiki with an amazing yoga teacher called Magda, who ingratiated me into her yogic world. Through her centre, I began to train and to meet more and more like-minded souls.

The more I officially trained, and focused on the lessons within *The Abundance Book*, the more I felt able to offer my services to people. I wasn't inundated with clients, but I also had enough to enable me to shift from surviving to a mindset that felt like it was thriving, but not just financially; I was beginning to flourish on all levels, mentally, emotionally, physically, and spiritually. I started to realise that today I have enough, that in the now, I AM prosperous.

With Magda I also trained in angelic reiki and became an Angelic Reiki Master. I also began to focus on the inspiration of the work of Tim Wheater and Lyz Cooper, who are both involved in the practice of sound therapy. I commenced this training, starting in the UK and then moved my learning more local. I was invited by Magda to offer sound baths and 1:1 sound healing therapy sessions at her yoga retreats.

More and more people began to learn about my work; some of them were hugely sceptical, but close friends supported me and became case studies. I began to get astounding results using a combination of sound and reiki, which led to friends talking to their friends about me. Dawn was one of my case study clients and she told everyone about how I'd helped her alleviate years of back pain. Her recommendation, then led to gaining more clients, including a local doctor and an 86-year-old gentleman who for over a year, has had a weekly combination of angelic reiki and sound therapy. He started from a place of not really believing in the modality of my work and now claims that whatever it is I do, it feels magical.

Regardless of all these amazing opportunities, I was still struggling to meet the cost of my rent and the cost of the HP car. I needed to reduce the cost of my rental fee by finding a new place to live and while my life was beginning to come together, I was really stressed about what I was going to do when the car needed to be returned to the garage.

The terms and conditions for the HP arrangement, required a deposit to be paid for the car, which was done while I was still with Ian. Our intention had been to use the car when visiting Spain. In addition, a monthly fee is also paid and then after a set period, which in this case was three years, the car is either returned, bought, or exchanged for a new HP deal.

I was earning, but I wasn't making enough money to pay the lease and to also put some aside to buy the current car or a replacement vehicle. This stressed me a lot. So as always, I spoke to God and focused on working with Him via guidance given in *The Abundance Book*. This time, I decided to be very specific about my wants and needs, ensuring that they matched with what was also in my heart, which is the centre of my soul.

I told God that I needed to reduce my rent by 100 euros a month. I told Him that I really wanted to have mountain views, so that I could feel more connected to Him on a daily basis. I wanted a driveway to park my car, so that I didn't have to lug my treatment couch, shopping or gas bottles up an exhaustive steep hill back to the town house. I wanted a spare room for friends to stay and a space to have a treatment room; I also suggested a garden would be nice too. I thought I was pushing my luck and asking for the impossible.

It's also important to add that I don't wish for it to sound as though I can just give God a shopping list of my needs and wants; it's conversations that relate to what is required on a deep soulful level. For most of the time, my request for help is fear driven and this is when I am sometimes given what I don't want to help me realise what I do want. My faith is a relationship of trust and respect.

I shared my wishes for a new place to live with my current landlady, Dawn, who without any judgement wanted to help and it was her who sourced me a new place to rent. When I went to visit my current home, I thought the outbuilding was what was on offer, but was astounded when I realised that it was the main house that was available to rent.

Prior to departing to live in Spain, I had spent hours looking at houses to buy and had fallen in love with the idea of living in a traditional white cortijo; the concept of living in an old place never appealed to Ian. But there I was, about to move home again, but this time to a traditional white cortijo, that had its own garden and driveway; orange, almond and carob trees. The rear of the house backs onto an olive grove that sits beneath a range of mountains.

Inside, there was a large kitchen, two bedrooms, which gave space for a friend to stay, a snug, which has doubled as my study. But the surprise didn't stop there; beneath the house was a casita, a granny flat, with two rooms and a shower room; a treatment and workshop space. To top all of that, the house was exactly 100 euros a month cheaper to rent; plus, it sits next door to a goat farm, which means that every day I hear the wonderful sound of goats and their tiny bells as they are herded along the mountain track. The house is truly a Divine gift.

Every day I also see Ibex, which continue to be a source of synchronicity, as they tend to appear whenever I am expressing any signs of doubt regarding my journey. One such day, I had just started writing this book and I was full of doubt regarding my worthiness to think I could write; I was also having doubts about the reality of my guidance. I then heard a noise on the roof above me, which sounded louder than what would be expected if birds were up there. So, I went to have a look and it was a male Ibex. The cortijo is set within the mountains so that the lower floor, the casita is below ground level, which means that areas of the garden is almost level with the roof. I returned to my desk to note that the time was 11:11.

Moving to the cortijo meant that I also began to really settle and to unpack and to embrace it as my home. I'd been living a transient life, almost out of a suitcase with Ian for a number of years. I had got so entrenched in his world and problems, that I hadn't sorted some of my own administrative affairs out for a long period of time. So, at last, I began to feel like it was time to put my life in order and to own the parts I'd been ignoring.

So, I started to sort through old paperwork, which I'd managed to grab when leaving Ian, and in it, I found various details on a number of small pensions belonging to me. Most of them were almost worthless, small contributions made while working in temping jobs for different government council offices. Nonetheless, I updated my contact details and filed the paperwork so that every small pension payment would count when needed.

Among the paperwork, I also found details of my TV pension. It was 20 years since I'd worked for the Leeds based company and I'd only been on staff for a short amount of time; therefore, I assumed that I hadn't accrued much. Nonetheless, getting my life in order, I updated my contact details and requested a statement for the pension account. To my surprise, I learnt that I was eligible to apply for a lump sum of over £10k and a small monthly payment of over £100. I'd almost forgotten about the pension, so it was like winning the lottery.

The company was very quick in dealing with my request and within a week, I was paid a lump sum that was enough to also resolve my car issue. I realise that I was only claiming what was rightfully mine, but in my mind, the fact that I was able to get this paperwork and the timing of the discovery, is too coincidental for me to claim that the pension came to me through my own long-term planning. It's also somewhat ironic that the career that Ian was so quick to condemn, has, after all these years, been a major source of support at a time when I needed it the most.

Each day I count my blessings and give gratitude for the beauty that is all around me. I'm not saying that I still don't have really bad days where everything in the world feels terrifying and all my plans for the future feel impossible. I still cry more now than I recall ever doing in the past; this leads to physical and emotional pain that affects me for days.

A friend called Brenda who escaped a similar relationship, advised me that it is normal to have these periods of what she feels are grieving the years that were lost and the dreams that were stolen. I hadn't envisaged that I would find myself on my own at this time of my life. And of course, while the decision to take the leap of faith was mine, or at least guided; I didn't foresee that one day the man who I thought I would love till the end of time, would be the man who I came to fear. The depth of his lies has robbed my soul of so many things, including the ability to trust and to know what love looks and feels like. The deep level of trauma bonding has left me with almost insatiable insecurities. So, the road to healing is long and winding.

Hence, it's importance to turn these glass half empty days, to ones where the glass is half full. To do this, I focus on and journal each day, all the things that have made me smile or given me joy, no matter how small. Whether it's a flowering cacti, a butterfly, a staff member helping at the checkout or a friend offering to buy a coffee; I log every moment and whenever I feel that life is unfair or sad or impossible, I read the list of things I am grateful for as a reminder that the good things far outweigh the parts of my life that still drag me down.

Since, I started to do this, the list of kindness from others is endless. The restaurant is closed for the months of January and February, which makes money tight, and the post-Christmas and colder period means that there is also a fall in holistic therapy clients.

Last year, 2023, I was so short of money that I was in a position of having to choose between buying petrol, food, or a gas bottle to heat the house. My elderly neighbour called me to tell me that the gas man was due to deliver and asked if I needed a bottle. I paused before responding, but never mentioned my dilemma. However, the neighbour sensed there was something wrong and offered to buy me a gas bottle and for me to pay them back when I could afford to. This same neighbour also made me a device to make it easier for me to attach the gas bottles to appliances. During this same period, a client left money on my doorstep in payment for a missed appointment: I hadn't asked them or expected them to do this. The money enabled me to buy gas, food, and petrol.

To take advantage of my time off from work, Lauren, who is now an adult and working in wave energy technology; invited me to take a 12-day break at her home in Barcelona. She understood my financial concerns and paid for my air ticket as a Christmas present. She was also aware that Ian had prevented me from collecting items from the marital home and that I was short of winter clothing including footwear. Since Lauren was a teenager, we have always worn the same size shoes, which made it easy for her to gift me a pair of winter boots. She also went to the trouble of buying my contact lenses because I simply couldn't afford them. It felt wonderful to gift her back some cash when I received my media pension.

What I've discovered is that the more I act from a place of gratitude and trust in God, the more that the spiritual awakening pathway positively reveals itself to me. I'm reaching a space whereby I know that everything is perfect, that with divine love and guidance, that there is no such things as scarcity. The more I trust, the more I radiate my own Light and raise my own vibration, which attracts more of the same wonderful energy. All of which impacts on my work and the love I have to give.

I have grown and my work in reality is just beginning because I am only just stepping into the true essence of myself now. I recently completed my 200 hour teacher training in the practice of Qigong, after being awarded a scholarship. I run regular wellness days for women and am sitting in a psychic development circle. The circle has afforded me some new like-minded friends.

I also learnt that a number of my neighbours at the cortijo are members of an orchestra; there is one opera singer, who also plays the cello, a pianist and Emily who plays the violin. I fell in love with the cello while at school, but my parents couldn't afford to pay for music lessons. Years later, I discovered a cello in a charity shop in Spain; it was priced at 100 euros.

I bought it. I later discovered that it wasn't a full size cello but is suitable for beginners. I started to have lessons with a gentle soul called Adrian, who advised that eventually I would need to acquire a full size cello. I thought about my priority to learn Spanish more so than the cello, which meant that I couldn't really justify the expense of buying a new musical instrument.

However, in the past month, a cello was gifted to me. It had belonged to the partner of one of the women who sits in the Spanish psychic development circle. It had belonged to their late daughter, a musician, who had died from a tumour. They'd wanted to gift the cello to someone with a good soul and after 11 years, there's that number again, chose to give the cello to me.

This extreme act of generosity helped me to put the rest of my life into perspective. A bright and promising young woman had lost her life and never had the opportunity to truly shine her Light. I'd delayed learning Spanish and the cello; I'd waited years to commence a new health regime, but in the darkness of the story behind the cello, is the inspiration to create a story of regrowth.

I am still awaiting news of a divorce and financial settlement. My initial lawyer Fernando returned to live and work in Granada and since his departure, I struggled to find a replacement. However, in the tiny hamlet I now live, Emily who plays the violin in the orchestra is also a lawyer. She heard about my case and even though divorce is not her area of expertise, she has still stepped forward to help me fight for my divorce and financial settlement. It's a community that keeps on giving. I AM a much loved member of my neighbourhood.

My relationship with God has also grown too. The journey to calling God my Holy Father was the realisation that I need only one provider and protector in my life, and that is Him working through me. I learnt that what I missed most in life was a father figure to watch over me, hence, God is the form I realised that I needed to heal what is missing within me, so he is the Holy Father, the guiding hand that I need to feel safe.

The synchronicity that led me to discovering the beautiful soul Manuel Angel, is no longer a therapist and client relationship. Instead, we are friends who share a deep spiritual love for each other, which allows us to grow and to feel safe. It's a relationship of unconditional love, that allows us to create a space to assist the other on their healing journey. It's a beautiful spiritual union.

I AM held, I AM loved, and I AM awakened.

This is my story, and the narrative will be different for each and every person who finds themselves in an abusive situation. I cannot stress enough, that if you are experiencing any form of abuse, no matter how silent it may seem, I urge you to find your own truth, to find your voice and to seek the help that you need. Know that you are capable of anything. Know that you are worthy of love and respect. Even with spiritual faith, I still needed the help of my earthbound friends to put my escape plan into action and for them to rescue me when needed.

> *'You can have a spiritual awakening and discover a new side of you at any age. And best of all, love can happen at any age. Life can just start to get exciting when you're in your 40s and 50s. You have to believe that.'*
>
> [Quote: Salma Hayek]

Footnote : at the time of going to publish this book in June '25, over two years since I took the leap of faith to leave Ian. He is now using a pseudonym on social media, claiming that he is an author specialising in self-help books. He claims to be a professor and specialist in the subjects of grief and anxiety. Speaking to a friend, who is also an advisor to victims of narcissistic abuse, it is yet not only another attempt to get into my head, but a means to mimicking my dreams and showing that he can surpass them. He has deliberately chosen subjects that have personally affected me. Ian has never expressed an interest in writing and thus, the speed at which he is churning out books on these specialist topics, one can only assume that they have been written by AI. I am determined to carry on with my own dreams regardless.

Appendix

As a reminder, I cannot stress enough the importance of not using the term 'narcissist' to offensively describe another person too freely; when the word becomes too generalised it devalues the seriousness of the subject matter. I would advise the same regarding any word that is used as a derogatory term, which is meant only for the use of describing or explaining accurately a situation or condition. If we use words too loosely and unwisely, we start to play a small part in silencing and normalising truly serious conditions or insidious behaviour.

There are many online resources that offer advice or insights into narcissistic abuse; I would advise that while these tools are helpful to support and further an understanding of the subject matter; using only a search engine to 'research' the subject and to form an opinion is not advisable. This would be the equivalent of using Google to diagnose a serious health condition, without seeking the advice of a doctor.

For the purpose of this book and to deepen my own healing, and understanding of the subject matter, I have carried out additional research. I have shared some of what I have learnt post-abuse in this book, but this by no means qualifies me as an expert on this subject; I am simply sharing my viewpoint of my own experience. My hope and intent is that if any part of my experience resonates with someone, that it inspires them to seek help.

In the vast list of available online resources that offer advice on the subject of narcissism, there are numerous red flags that have been pinpointed to help recognise narcissistic characteristics. Again, anyone who displays any of those listed is not necessarily a narcissist. From subtle manipulation to grandiose self-importance, the hallmarks of narcissism, can be as elusive as they are damaging, leaving the victim wondering if they are dealing with a narcissist or someone with an inflated ego.

The most extensive list I found of potential red flag warnings is one provided by www.grace-being.com; I have no affiliation with this site, other than to credit them for this list and explanation of terms used within the chapters.

The main red flags highlighted on this site include:

1. Love Bombing
2. Grandiose Self Image
3. Lack of Accountability
4. Charming
5. Controlling
6. Quick to Commit
7. Entitlement
8. Gaslighting
9. Frequent Lies
10. Lack of Empathy
11. Exploitative
12. Manipulative
13. Excessive Need for admiration
14. Jealousy
15. Quick to Anger
16. Plays the Victim
17. Double Standards
18. Sense of Perfection
19. Frequent Interruptions
20. Belittling Humour
21. Inconsistent Behaviour
22. Twists Conversations
23. Neglectful
24. Competitive
25. Disregards Others Feelings
26. Sees Others as an Extension of Self
27. Unrealistic Expectations
28. Guilt Tripping
29. Need to Win Arguments

30. Refusal to Acknowledge any Wrongdoing
31. Devaluation
32. Isolation from Others
33. Inflating Achievements
34. Possessiveness
35. Erratic Behaviour

In the writing of this book, I have overlapped some of the red flags; for example, in my personal experience, I chose to link devaluation with exploitation, likewise, I view grandiose self-image and entitlement as being similar when describing Ian. But clearly, every person and every case will be different.

ABOUT THE AUTHOR:

Sally Jayne lives in southern Spain, where she works part-time as a sous chef in a rustic mountain restaurant. When she's not busy prepping food, she offers 1:1 holistic therapies that focus on helping her clients reconnect with their natural state of flow using a combination of reiki and sound therapy. Sally Jayne is a registered Angelic Reiki Master, Angel Teacher and has recently graduated to teach Qigong.

Sally Jayne is currently working on her second book, Silent Abuse: *The Early Years*. In this book, the author explores the traumatic and damaging childhood that created the perfect qualities of people-pleasing and empath, for narcissistic abuse.